BIRTH OF THE CONSTITUTION

S0-BND-313

This book tells how a group of unusually talented men joined in 1787 to create a constitution for a new United States and what the Constitution has meant over the years.

The book begins with the events leading up to the Constitutional Convention: the Newburgh Conspiracy (when Continental officers proposed taking over the government), how the colonies were governed after the end of the Revolutionary War, and the proposal that a meeting be held to revise the Articles of Confederation, which was then governing the colonies.

The second part describes the Constitutional Convention itself: the character of the men who came to the Convention, how the big states wanted one plan and the small ones another, and how compromises paved the way to a solution.

The third part tells how the Constitution was created as a living document: how a system of checks and balances was created among the legislative, executive, and judicial branches, how the Bill of Rights was added, how the Supreme Court has interpreted the Constitution, and how the Constitution has been changed by later Amendments. The author gives the text of each Amendment and explains its meaning and significance. For example, he explains how the Supreme Court has interpreted the Fourteenth Amendment as giving individuals the right of "due process" not only against

continued on back flap

BIRTH OF THE CONSTITUTION

EDMUND LINDOP

J
342.73
LIN
cop.2

ENSLOW PUBLISHERS, INC.

Bloy St. & Ramsey Ave.	P.O. Box 38
Box 777	Aldershot
Hillside, N.J. 07205	Hants GU12 6BP
U.S.A.	U.K.

31861

Copyright © 1987 by Edmund Lindop

All rights reserved.

No part of this book may be reproduced by any means without the written permission of the publisher.

Library of Congress Cataloging in Publication Data

Lindop, Edmund.
    Birth of the Constitution.

    Bibliography: p.
    Includes index.
    Summary: Discusses the creating of the Constitution and the very few changes that have been made in it during the past 200 years.
    1. United   States—Constitutional   history—Juvenile literature. 2. United   States. Constitutional Convention (1787)—Juvenile   literature. [1.   United   States—Constitutional History. 2. United States. Constitutional Convention (1787)] I. Title.
KF4541.Z9L56   1987   342.73'029   86-13380
ISBN 0-89490-135-4, hardcover   347.30229
ISBN 0-89490-158-3, paperback

Printed in the United States of America

10 9 8 7 6 5 4 3 2 1

Illustration Credits:
American Philosophical Society, pp. 47, 66; Architect of the Capitol, p. 58; Independence National Historical Park Collection, pp. 8, 41, 48, 51, 70, 72, 77; Library of Congress, pp. 85, 122, 127; Museum of Fine Arts, Boston, p. 81; Museum of the City of New York, p. 21; National Geographic Society Photographer, courtesy of U.S. Capitol Historical Society, p. 97; National Portrait Gallery, Smithsonian Institution, Washington, D.C., p. 101; courtesy of the Pennsylvania Academy of Fine Arts, p. 45; Picture Collection, The Branch Libraries, The New York Public Library, p. 86; courtesy of Supreme Court of the United States, p. 63; Virginia Museum of Fine Arts, gift of Colonel and Mrs. Edgar W. Garbisch, p. 53; Wide World Photos, Inc., p. 113; copyright Yale University Art Gallery: "Surrender of Lord Cornwallis" by John Trumbull, p. 13; copyright Yale University Art Gallery: "The Declaration of Independence" by John Trumbull, p. 24; copyright Yale University Art Gallery: "Alexander Hamilton" by John Trumbull, p. 35.

To Esther and Laurie, with love

Acknowledgment

The author thanks Dr. Robert J. Steamer of the Political Science Department at the University of Massachusetts for reviewing the entire manuscript and for making valuable suggestions.

Contents

The Constitutional Convention met in 1787 in Independence Hall (then called the Philadelphia State House), where the Declaration of Independence had been written eleven years before.

PART ONE

YEARS OF CRISES

1

The Newburgh Conspiracy

The war for independence was nearly over. More than sixteen months had passed since Lord Cornwallis had surrendered at Yorktown. His band, according to legend, had played "The World Turned Upside Down" to mark the end of Great Britain's control over its American colonies. British troops still occupied New York City, but all the fighting had ceased. The draft of a peace treaty had been signed at Paris, and it was now on its way to the American Congress at Philadelphia.

It had been eight long years since those few brave farmers at Lexington and Concord had started the American Revolution by firing "the shots heard round the world." Eight long years of suffering and sacrifice, of going without enough food and warm clothing for weeks on end, of feeling pain and facing death on battlefields turned crimson with young men's blood.

But those dark days of agony finally had ended. The killing had stopped. And Americans were free at last! Free to shape their own future, free to forge their own nation. Moreover, Americans were soon to gain from Britain much more land than they dreamed they would own. No longer would they be confined to a narrow strip of land hugging the Atlantic coast. Britain was giving them all of its territory west of the

Appalachian Mountains, except Canada. American pioneers could expand westward across half a continent—all the way to the muddy waters of the Mississippi River.

There was much rejoicing among the delegates to the American Congress assembled at Philadelphia. They could hardly wait to ratify (approve) the peace treaty ending the lengthy war. The Congress in which these delegates served was not the same Congress that meets today in Washington, D.C. The United States, as we know it, had not yet been born. Americans at that time were governed under a document known as the Articles of Confederation, and the ruling body was called the Confederation Congress.

Some of the Americans who had fought in the Revolutionary War, however, were not as happy as the congressmen in Philadelphia. One group of disgruntled army officers was stationed at Newburgh, New York, in a camp nestled above the Hudson River. General George Washington was at this camp, and he was concerned because some of his most trusted and capable officers were seething with anger.

In January 1783 they had sent a committee to Philadelphia to demand some money from the Confederation Congress. The committee claimed that the officers had not been paid their wages for months, that their food and clothing allowances were long overdue, and that they had been promised a pension but no plans had yet been made to set up this fund.

The members of Congress listened sympathetically to the committee's pleas, but they replied that there was not enough money in the treasury to meet any of the officers' demands. Moreover, Congress had no power to tax the people or the states, so its sources of funds were few and very unreliable. Discouraged and resentful, the committee sent word back to Newburgh that its cause seemed hopeless.

On March 10, 1783, two unsigned messages were quietly circulated among the officers at Newburgh. One of them proposed that unless Congress could be forced to grant their requests, the officers would refuse to disband, "retire to some unsettled country," and leave Congress without an army. The other message called for a meeting the next day at which the officers could plan their conspiracy.

When British troops under Lord Cornwallis surrendered to General George Washington at Yorktown in October 1781, Americans felt confident that they would win their long struggle for independence.

When General Washington saw these two messages, he was appalled. Whoever had written these papers wanted the army to desert Congress, leave the people defenseless, and set up its own state in the West. Washington knew that such a conspiracy posed a dangerous threat to the young, struggling government at Philadelphia. It could spawn a second revolution, even before the first one had officially ended. What such a revolution might do to the government no one could say. But Washington feared that it might overthrow Congress and lead to a military dictatorship.

This was not the first time that the general from Mount Vernon had been confronted with the idea that the military might take over the government. Back in the summer of 1782 Colonel Lewis Nicola, who headed an army regiment, had suggested that America become a monarchy with Commander in Chief Washington as the first king. This suggestion infuriated Washington, who wrote in his reply to Nicola, "Be assured, sir, no occurrence in the course of the war has given me more [unpleasant] sensations." Then he scolded the colonel severely.

Washington had dismissed Nicola's proposal as the foolish notion of one troublesome agitator. But now he had to cope with a whole corps of officers furious at Congress because it would not give them the money they felt they deserved. The commander in chief who for so many years had served alongside these officers felt great compassion for them. Yes, these brave comrades certainly were entitled to everything they had requested of Congress. But even more important than their own needs was the future course of the land they had fought so hard to free. Would America be governed democratically by the people? Or, like most other countries in the world at that time, would it fall under the rule of the sword and the scepter?

Washington knew he was facing a crisis as grave as any that he had met on the battlefield. He had to act swiftly—and decisively. So he issued an order canceling the meeting scheduled for March 11, which had been called without his permission. Instead, General Washington summoned the officers to a special meeting on March 15. One sentence in the order read, "The officer in rank will be pleased to preside and report the result of the deliberations to the Commander-in-Chief."

At first Washington had not planned to go to the meeting himself. But the more he thought about what might happen there, the more certain he was that he should attend the meeting and express his own strong feelings to the officers. Otherwise, they might plot some drastic action that he would be powerless to prevent.

On the morning of Saturday, March 15, the officers of the Continental Army gathered in a large wooden building called the Temple, which was used for church services on Sundays and for dances at other times. The chief conspirators looked around the spacious room and, not seeing their commander in chief, felt relieved. But when the meeting was about to begin, a door at the back of the room opened, and in strode General Washington.

Shoulders erect, head held high, he walked briskly to the speakers' platform. As he looked out at the audience, Washington may have felt his heart pounding. For the first time since he had assumed command of the Continental Army, he saw in the faces of many officers embarrassment and even resentment.

Washington began his remarks by explaining that at the time he had issued the order for this meeting, he had not intended to be present. Then he apologized for changing his mind. He said that he had decided to tell his officers how he felt about the unsigned messages that had been circulated throughout the Newburgh camp.

First, he lashed out at the anonymous author who had proposed that the army either move into the wilderness and establish a separate country or force Congress at gunpoint to grant its demands. "This dreadful alternative," he exclaimed, "of either deserting our country in the extremest hour of her distress or turning our arms against it . . . has something so shocking in it, that humanity revolts at the idea."

He continued: ". . . let me entreat you, gentlemen, on your part, not to take any measure which, viewed in the calm light of reason, will lessen the dignity and sully the glory you have hitherto maintained." Then he begged the officers to be patient, to have faith in their government. In time, he promised, Congress would find some way to pay them.

Washington had completed what he planned to say, but he sensed that the chill in the Temple still had not thawed. The faces he knew so well still looked troubled and sullen. Then he reached in his pocket and pulled out a paper. This, he said, was a letter from a member of Congress that would explain what that body was trying to do and how great its problems were.

The officers squirmed impatiently in their seats as the general began to read. He stumbled through the first few sentences, struggling over nearly every word. Then he paused as if bewildered, and the paper shook in his hands. The men in the audience were puzzled. What was wrong with the general? they wondered.

Washington fumbled in his waistcoat pocket and pulled out a pair of glasses. Few of the men had ever seen him wearing glasses, because he used them only in the privacy of his office.

"Gentlemen," he said softly, "you will permit me to put on my spectacles, for I have not only grown gray but almost blind in the service of my country."

That simple statement accomplished what none of his earlier words had been able to do. It moved the officers deeply, and tears welled in their eyes. Again they felt a tremendous surge of affection for the commander who had led them all so far and long.

After Washington read the congressman's letter, he quickly left the hall. A committee of officers then drew up a resolution that expressed their confidence in the justice of Congress, and it was passed unanimously. Later, with the help of the wartime financier Robert Morris, Congress managed to raise part of the money the officers requested.

Congress's troubles, however, were far from over. In June 1783 about eighty soldiers stationed at Lancaster, Pennsylvania, mutinied against their officers. They marched on Philadelphia, determined to use force if necessary to get their back pay. When they reached the capital city, the mutineers were joined by some five hundred state troops from the Philadelphia barracks.

At this time both the Confederation Congress and the Executive Council that headed the Pennsylvania state government met in a building called the State House. On the morning of June 21, a large group of angry mutineers surrounded the State House. Some of them broke windows and pushed their bayonets inside. They cursed and snarled insults at the frightened legislators and threatened to storm the building.

Alexander Hamilton, a delegate to Congress, hurried to the meeting room of the Executive Council and urged John Dickinson, the president (governor) of Pennsylvania, to call out the state militia immediately. The lives of the congressmen were in great danger, he exclaimed. But Dickinson just shook his head and said he could do nothing. Taking Hamilton to a window, he pointed at the restless mob outside and said it included many militiamen. If he called out the rest of the militia, large numbers of these soldiers probably would join the mutineers, too.

Since Congress could not be defended, the delegates slipped out of the back door of the State House and fled Philadelphia. About ten days later they met again at Princeton, New Jersey. Later they moved to Annapolis, Maryland, then to Trenton, New Jersey, and finally to New York City.

Washington described the mutiny at Philadelphia as "infamous and outrageous." He was deeply troubled by the terrible humiliation Congress had suffered.

Many Americans shared Washington's concern. They were disturbed by the same haunting questions: Could they have faith in a government so weak that its leaders flee from its own soldiers? Could this government possibly survive?

2

A Rope of Sand

Before the Revolutionary War each of the thirteen colonies had its own government with a legislature and a governor. All of the colonies were part of the British Empire, but they were not united in any other way.

During a period of more than a century, the colonial assemblies had gradually gained the power to levy taxes, spend money, and make laws to govern themselves. Before 1763 the British Parliament held only a loose rein over the colonies. But following the French and Indian War that ended in 1763, Britain began tightening its rule in the American colonies. The war had been very expensive, and the people in England already were paying heavy taxes. The American colonists, Parliament concluded, should bear part of the cost of this war and should also pay for the British troops who would defend them against possible Indian attacks in the future. So in 1765 Parliament imposed a stamp tax on the colonists. The tax was put on fifty-four kinds of articles, including newspapers, almanacs, playing cards, dice, and all legal documents.

The colonists were furious when they learned about the new stamp tax, and many vowed not to pay it. Since they had no delegates in Parliament, Americans throughout the colonies raised a clamor that this was "taxation without representation." In Massachusetts James Otis called for an intercolonial protest meeting to plan some unified action against the new form of taxation. This meeting, known as the Stamp Act Congress, took place in October 1765. Nine state legislatures were represented, and the others sent word that they approved of the meeting.

The delegates drew up a set of resolutions condemning the tax and sent petitions to the British king and Parliament. These petitions demanded that the Stamp Act be repealed. Even more important, they organized a general boycott of British-made goods, and large numbers of colonists decided not to buy anything that came from Britain.

The boycott was very effective, and British merchants, whose sales to the colonists dropped off sharply, besieged Parliament with pleas to end the unpopular tax. Under such strong pressure, Parliament repealed the Stamp Act in 1766. The first protest meeting of American colonists had achieved its goal!

The second protest meeting occurred after the famous "Boston Tea Party" in 1773. To demonstrate against the hated tax on tea, a band of colonists, slightly disguised as Indians, boarded the tea ships in Boston harbor and tossed 342 crates of tea overboard. Angered by this action, the British Parliament passed a series of harsh laws that included closing the port of Boston until the tea was paid for and restricting the right of self-government in the colony of Massachusetts.

These new laws, which Americans called the Intolerable Acts, unleashed a torrent of rage, not only in Massachusetts but in the other colonies, too. The Intolerable Acts convinced many Americans that Parliament wanted to destroy their rights and that what had been done to Massachusetts could easily happen elsewhere. Again the colonists felt a strong need to hold an intercolonial meeting and form a united defense against the abuses of the British government.

In September 1774 all the colonies except Georgia sent delegates to the First Continental Congress in Philadelphia. This Congress demanded that the British government end the Intolerable Acts and declared that all trade with England would be cut off until the detested acts were repealed. Furthermore, the Congress denounced every step taken by Britain since 1763 to raise money or tighten control in America as

This Currier and Ives print shows the artists' conception of the famous Boston Tea Party.

violations of colonial charters and the colonists' rights as British citizens. Yet, in spite of their strong stand against British policies, most of the delegates to the First Continental Congress still considered themselves loyal subjects of the king and expressed their devotion to George III. Before adjourning, the delegates announced that they would meet again the following year.

This time, however, the British government did not give in to the colonists' demands, and by May 1775, when the Second Continental Congress assembled, the first shots of the Revolution had been fired at Lexington and Concord. Americans were now at war with Britain, but as yet they had neither a declaration of independence nor a unified central government.

Some of the delegates to the Second Continental Congress were reluctant to cut all ties with the mother country. After all, Britain had a powerful army and navy, while the colonists had no standing army or large fleet of warships. The Americans' struggle for freedom might end in a crushing defeat, and then all who lost their lives in the war would have died in vain. But even if the colonists were victorious, was it wise to give up the protection of a mighty empire for an uncertain future in which thirteen relatively weak states had to fend for themselves? Also, the Americans could not overlook the other ties that bound them to Britain—the same language, a common literature, and a shared heritage of democratic laws and traditions.

So for many months the Continental Congress dodged the question of whether to commit the colonists to a complete break with Britain. Finally, on June 7, 1776, Richard Henry Lee, a delegate from Virginia, made the motion: "These colonies are and of right ought to be free and independent states." The members of Congress then realized that if Lee's motion was adopted, some form of central unified government would be needed to carry on the war with Britain. So two committees were appointed. One was to draft a declaration of independence; the other was to prepare the articles of union.

On July 2, Lee's motion passed in Congress, and two days later the delegates adopted the Declaration of Independence, eloquently written by Thomas Jefferson. Eight days after the Declaration of Independence was adopted, a thirteen-member committee presented to Congress the first draft of what was to become the Articles of Confederation.

But the Articles faced rough sledding in the Second Continental Congress. For many months their provisions were heatedly debated. Conflicts had to be resolved and compromises had to be reached before Congress finally adopted the Articles in November 1777 and sent them to the states for ratification (approval).

All of the legislatures of the thirteen states had to ratify the Articles before they could become the framework of a new government. Nearly four and one-half years passed before the thirteenth state, Maryland, ratified the Articles on March 1, 1781. By that time the war was nearly over!

What powers did the first government of the United States have? It had the power to wage war and make treaties, raise armies and navies, borrow money, manage affairs with the Indians, establish a postal system, and coin its own money. To finance its operations, Congress could request money from the states and sell public lands.

The two chief accomplishments of the Articles of Confederation government concerned western lands. Its Congress passed the Land Ordinance of 1785, a law that provided an orderly method to survey and sell the government-owned lands north of the Ohio River. The so-called Northwest Ordinance of 1787 was even more significant. It provided for the political development of the entire region bounded by the Ohio River, the Great Lakes, and the Mississippi River.

This Northwest Territory was to be divided into not less than three nor more than five states. When the population of any area within this vast territory reached sixty thousand, its people could organize a new state that would be admitted to the Union on terms of full equality with the original states. This was something new; never before had a country promised full equality to its colonies or territories and set up a formal plan for fulfilling this promise. In time the present states of Ohio, Indiana, Illinois, Michigan, and Wisconsin were carved from the Northwest Territory.

Members of the Second Continental Congress come forward to sign the Declaration of Independence in July 1776, more than a year after hostilities began at Lexington and Concord.

The Northwest Ordinance supplied the model, later followed in other regions, for admitting new states to the Union on equal terms. It also declared that slavery was forbidden in the Northwest Territory, thus making the Ohio River a boundary between future free and slave states.

Except for its action dealing with western lands and its acceptance of the treaty ending the war with Britain, the Articles Congress had few successes. This was chiefly because the men who had drawn up its charter did not want their new government to have much power. They were very fearful of a strong central government. Having thrown off one tyrannical master, the British Parliament, they did not intend to put themselves under another.

So each state could and did put its own interests above those of the nation. In fact, the Confederation Congress could do only those limited things which its charter specifically said it could do. The individual states had the power to do everything else. Moreover, Congress could not force the states to carry out any of its decisions; it had to depend on the voluntary cooperation of the states.

Under the Articles there was a one-house Congress in which each state had a single vote. The state governments paid their delegates' salaries out of their own funds and completely controlled their votes in Congress. Every bill that Congress passed had to be approved by nine of the thirteen states. But even when two-thirds of the states agreed on a measure and made it a law, the national government had no way to compel the other states to obey it.

The Articles government had no executive branch to carry out its laws. There was no real president, as we have today, empowered to put laws into operation, originate treaties, promote policies, and guide the course of the nation. And there was no national court system to enforce the laws made by Congress and punish those who broke them. Justice was served only by state courts that dealt entirely with cases involving state laws.

During the Confederation period, the government had serious problems conducting foreign affairs. While the British agreed to receive John Adams as minister from the United States, they had such a low opinion of the Confederation government that they refused to send it a minister in return. The British sarcastically claimed that they did not know whether to send one envoy or thirteen! Also, American ships were banned from the rich trade of the British West Indies and allowed to enter English ports only with the products of their home states.

The British were so unimpressed by the strength of the new American government that they would not carry out in full the terms of the treaty ending the Revolutionary War. This treaty called for the British to turn over to the Americans some trading posts and forts in the Great Lakes region and the Ohio Valley. But after the war the British refused to surrender these places, claiming as their excuse that the Americans had not fulfilled some promises they had made in the same treaty. The American delegates who signed the treaty had agreed that British merchants could collect the colonists' prewar debts by suing in American courts. They also agreed that Congress would urge the states to end the persecution of Loyalists who had supported Britain during the war. But the states simply ignored the recommendations from the Articles government to treat British merchants and Loyalists fairly, and Congress had no power to force the states to obey its requests.

Relations with Spain suffered during this period, too. The Spanish disagreed with Americans about the southeastern boundary of the United States, supplied Indian tribes in the Southeast with arms, hired some citizens of the United States to act as Spanish secret agents, and refused to make a treaty that would grant Americans free navigation of the Mississippi River. Many western farmers, whose products could not be carried profitably over the mountains to the Atlantic coast, depended on sending their goods on rafts and flatboats down the Mississippi River and then transferring them at New Orleans to oceangoing ships. But the Spanish put a high tax on the goods that were reloaded at New Orleans, and the westerners were furious at Congress for being unable to make a treaty with Spain that would end this taxation.

The most dismal failure of the Confederation Congress to deal with foreign affairs was seen in the harsh treatment American ships received at the hands of the Barbary pirates. These pirates, who came from four North African states along the Mediterranean coast, captured the ships and crews of all nations that did not pay them an annual tribute, or bribe. American ships that entered the Mediterranean Sea became the targets of vicious pirate attacks. Having neither the money for tribute nor a navy for defense, Congress was powerless to prevent American shipping from being forced out of the Mediterranean.

Congress was not able to regulate foreign trade or trade among the states. Even though it was given the power to make trade treaties, the states did not have to accept their provisions. New York, Pennsylvania, New Hampshire, North Carolina, and Rhode Island each adopted separate laws to regulate their foreign trade. Massachusetts would not allow its products to be carried by British ships. Maryland imposed higher tariffs on trade with Britain than with other countries, and South Carolina decreed a 2.5 percent tariff on all foreign products.

Each state also could pass laws taxing goods from other states. New York, for example, taxed firewood from New Jersey. Moreover, New Jersey residents who bought foreign goods that came into the country through the port of New York City had to pay taxes on them to New York State. These interstate taxes caused hard feelings throughout the country.

Even more serious were the angry arguments over state boundaries. Parts of the present state of Vermont were claimed by New York, New Hampshire, and Massachusetts. The people of Vermont were so frustrated by these disputes that some of them even felt that rejoining the British Empire would be better than being the prize that their greedy neighbors quarreled about. Farther to the south, Connecticut and Pennsylvania settlers came to blows over a contested region called the Wyoming Valley. The Pennsylvania militia attacked Connecticut farmers in the valley, seizing their lands and killing those settlers who resisted.

Another source of trouble among the states was the lack of a single currency, or kind of money, that would have the same value throughout the country. Gold and silver were very scarce, so the states had to print their own paper money. These currencies differed in value from state to state and often were worthless outside the states that issued them.

Debt-ridden farmers wanted more money in circulation so that they could get higher prices for their products. So in Rhode Island and North Carolina these farmers gained control of the state legislatures and forced their governments to print huge amounts of paper money. When this happened, the value of the money declined sharply. Merchants began refusing their own state's currency. In Rhode Island the legislature then passed a law to force the merchants of that state to accept its paper money at face value. Some merchants reacted to this law by closing their businesses or demanding that customers use the barter system and exchange their goods for the things they wanted to buy. This caused many farmers to quit selling their food products to towns. Confusion and fear spread throughout Rhode Island, and this small state's economy was in danger of total collapse.

Getting enough money was the most serious immediate problem for the nation, too. Without being allowed to tax either the states or the people, the Confederation simply could not perform the services that were expected of a national government. For example, it had the power to wage war, but it did not have the money to provide for an army or navy.

Since taxation was not permitted under the Articles charter, the only way to change this situation was to amend the charter. But the charter could be amended only by a unanimous vote of all thirteen states. In 1781 Congress proposed that the charter be amended to permit a national tariff of 5 percent on imports. Twelve states voted to accept the amendment, but Rhode Island said no, so the will of the other twelve states was frustrated. In 1783 Congress proposed an annual tax payment of $1.5 million from the states, to be apportioned (divided) on the basis of the population of the states. This time New York cast the single no vote that doomed the measure.

Added to all the Confederation's problems was the dim view that many citizens took of their national government. Outstanding leaders in many states refused to serve as congressmen; they much preferred holding offices in their state governments. Those who did become delegates to Congress frequently were absent from its sessions. Often Congress did not have enough members present to conduct any business. And the most humiliating blow of all occurred in 1783 when some unpaid soldiers mutinied and drove Congress out of Philadelphia.

It is no wonder that George Washington sadly described the national government as a "rope of sand" and observed that "the Confederation appears to me to be a shadow without substance."

3

The Road to Philadelphia

There would be no solution to the nation's problems as long as the states continued squabbling and refused to cooperate. But how could thirteen separate, independent states, fearful of losing their power and freedom, cast aside their differences and work together as a unified team? The road that led to the creation of a stronger union had never been traveled before, and it was strewn with pitfalls and obstacles that no one could foresee.

In March 1785 two states forged an agreement that showed all Americans the benefits that could be gained from cooperation. For a long time Maryland and Virginia had been quarreling about navigation rights on the Potomac River and Chesapeake Bay—waters the two states shared in common. How should they divide the tariffs collected on foreign products shipped up the Potomac to customers in both states? How should these states share the cost of maintaining lighthouses, beacons, and buoys? Should Virginia ships be allowed to dock at Maryland ports without paying fees and vice versa?

Both state governments agreed to send representatives to a conference that would deal with these problems. It was scheduled to be held at Alexandria, Virginia, but George Washington invited the delegates to meet instead at his comfortable Mount Vernon estate. The meeting began on March

25, 1785, and ended on March 28. During these few days all of the two states' navigation questions were settled, and the delegates went beyond their original plans and made additional agreements. They declared the Potomac River "a common High Way" not only to the citizens of Virginia and Maryland but to those of the United States and to all other persons "in amity [friendship] with the said states." The representatives further recommended that the current money of the two states have the same value and that duties on imports and exports be the same for both states.

One exciting idea that the delegates discussed was the possible construction of canals to link the Potomac River with the Ohio River and the Chesapeake Bay with the Delaware River. Such a project would join the coastal regions to lands much farther inland by a system of interlocking waterways. It was strongly approved by General Washington, who was personally interested in developing western lands.

This plan to unite East and West by waterways would also involve Pennsylvania and Delaware, so Maryland proposed that these additional states be invited to take part in a broader discussion of questions affecting trade and commerce. The idea of expanding the discussion of trade regulations to include more states greatly interested James Madison of Virginia, who believed that the national government must be made more powerful. So this ardent nationalist persuaded the Virginia legislature to go a step further and call for a convention of all the states "to consider how far a uniform system in their commercial regulations may be necessary to their common interest and their permanent harmony."

Madison's strategy was obvious. Like Washington, he believed that the national government was too weak to survive in its present form. So when he called for establishing a "uniform system" of trade, he was, in effect, demanding congressional control of commerce among the states. If this could be accomplished, it would be a giant stride toward strengthening the national government.

The interstate convention requested by Virginia met in September 1786 at Annapolis, Maryland. But Madison's hope that this convention would produce a more powerful union was shattered when just twelve delegates from only five states (Virginia, New York, New Jersey, Pennsylvania, and Delaware) arrived for the meeting. Obviously, nothing could be done at this conference to establish a "uniform system" of trade when only five of the thirteen states were represented. Madison was deeply disappointed.

Nevertheless, the Annapolis convention was not a complete failure. Most of the twelve delegates were nationalists who shared Madison's belief that the Confederation government was in grave peril of falling apart. The most outspoken member of this group was Alexander Hamilton, a brilliant young delegate from New York. Before the Annapolis convention adjourned, Hamilton prepared a report asking that all of the states appoint delegates to meet at Philadelphia on the second Monday of the following May. Hamilton's report contained a thunderbolt that would shake the very foundation of the Confederation and lead to the birth of our present government. He advocated that the delegates at the proposed convention go far beyond the discussion of trade regulations. They must also "devise such further provisions as shall [should] appear to them necessary to render the constitution of the federal government adequate to the exigencies [urgent needs] of the union." So Hamilton was laying the groundwork for a convention that might propose radical changes in the central government.

Before the men at the Annapolis convention left for home, they unanimously approved Hamilton's report and sent a copy to each of the state governments and another copy to the Congress. Naturally, they were concerned about how Hamilton's bold report would be received in state legislatures that had selfishly clung to every ounce of their power. Would they consent to send delegates to a convention that might strip them of many of their jealously guarded powers? And would the Confederation Congress give its blessing to a conference that might issue its own death warrant?

Events in far-off Massachusetts unexpectedly played into the nationalists' hands. The Massachusetts legislature levied high taxes and, unlike the legislatures of seven other states, refused to print unsupported paper money to provide more currency. Debt-ridden farmers in the western part of the state could not meet their mortgage payments; the courts were seizing their land and sometimes putting them in jail. In September 1786 some angry farmers started an armed rebellion. About six hundred insurgents tried to prevent the state supreme court from meeting in Springfield and threatened to capture the national government's arsenal there. Massachusetts called out its militia, and the armed farmers had to fall back.

The rebellion continued, however, under the leadership of Daniel Shays, a former army captain in the Revolutionary War. More disgruntled farmers joined the cause. The governor of Massachusetts frantically appealed to the national government for troops. But no help came from Congress, which had only about seven hundred soldiers, most of them stationed far from Massachusetts. So the state had to beg for money from some of its wealthier citizens to hire enough soldiers to put down the insurrection. Eventually, in February 1787 a greatly enlarged Massachusetts militia routed the rebels, capturing Shays and the other leaders. (They were sentenced to death but later pardoned.)

Word of the rebellion in Massachusetts spread throughout the states. Many Americans, especially those who owned considerable amounts of land or large businesses, were terrified. The same conditions that had led to the insurrection in Massachusetts existed in other states, too. Similar rebellions could break out anytime anywhere. If the national government could not crush Shays' Rebellion, there was no reason to expect that it could maintain law and order in other parts of the country.

Prodded by Madison and news of the rebellion in Massachusetts, the Virginia legislature took quick action on Hamilton's Annapolis report and selected delegates to attend the proposed convention in Philadelphia. One by one the other states appointed delegates—all except Rhode Island, whose government was dominated by debt-burdened farmers and never sent any representatives to the Constitutional Convention.

Alexander Hamilton was an outspoken advocate of a strong national government.

The Annapolis report reached Congress on September 20, 1786, but the legislators were in no hurry to act on a proposal that might drastically alter their own futures. Five months of dreary wrangling ensued, but after seven states had selected delegates to the convention, the congressmen realized that the meeting was going to take place, with or without their approval. So on February 21, 1787, Congress officially recognized the convention, thus giving it the appearance of legality. But in its message to the states Congress declared that the convention's authority would be greatly restricted. The delegates to the Philadelphia conference, Congress stated, would meet "for the sole and express purpose of revising the Articles of Confederation."

Revise the Articles of Confederation. Would this be sufficient to save the Union from disintegration? No, agreed fervent nationalists like Hamilton, Madison, and Washington. It was impossible to revise the Articles without the unanimous consent of all thirteen states—and this could not be obtained. (Since Rhode Island refused even to send delegates to the Philadelphia convention, it and probably other states could not be expected to confirm any amendments proposed by the convention.) Nothing short of replacing the weak Confederation with a new, much stronger form of government would guarantee the continuation of the Union. But this daring belief could not yet be widely publicized by the nationalists. Neither Congress nor the majority of American citizens were ready to accept a new government that would have the authority to do many things that the Confederation Congress could not do.

So those who favored radical changes that would, in effect, call for a second American revolution had to tone down their public remarks for the time being. Otherwise, the Philadelphia convention would have been doomed to failure, even before it began.

PART TWO

DAYS OF DECISIONS

4

An Assembly of Demigods

All of the thirteen states except Rhode Island were represented at the Philadelphia convention in 1787. Only fifty-five of the appointed seventy-four delegates undertook the journey to Philadelphia, which was then the nation's largest city with a population of about forty-five thousand. They drifted in on their own schedules, and though the convention was scheduled to open on May 14, the last representative did not arrive until August 6.

On May 14 the only delegations present were from Pennsylvania and Virginia. The convention had to delay its opening session until May 25, which was the first day when delegates from a majority of states (seven) were present. From then until it finished its work on September 17, there was a steady coming and going of delegates. Some of the men slipped out of Philadelphia on business errands or family matters and then returned; others left the unfinished business of the convention and never came back. Only a small, dedicated group of about twenty members were rarely absent; the average daily attendance of delegates was a little more than thirty.

While some of the delegates were less faithful than others about attending the meetings, the Philadelphia convention brought together many of the wisest, best-educated, and most prominent leaders in the American states. A large number of them already had extensive public service and held a variety of high government positions. Thomas Jefferson, who was not a delegate and was then serving as the American minister to France, described the Philadelphia convention as "an assembly of demigods." (Demigods are persons who seem to have godlike powers.)

Seventeen delegates besides George Washington had been American officers in the Revolutionary War, and four of these had served on his staff. Another thirteen had been militia officers. Eight had been members of one or both of the Continental Congresses, eight had signed the Declaration of Independence, and six had signed the Articles of Confederation. Thirty-nine had served in the Confederation Congress, fourteen had been state judges or state attorneys, and seven were governors or ex-governors. An occupational breakdown shows that over thirty had legal training, thirteen were planters or large-scale farmers, four were college presidents or professors, eight were merchants, and three were physicians.

In an age when only a very small percentage of the population received higher education, twenty-nine of the delegates were college graduates. Ten had earned their degrees at the College of New Jersey (now Princeton), and others were graduates of Harvard, Yale, William and Mary, King's College (now Columbia), the College of Philadelphia (now the University of Pennsylvania), Oxford, and the Universities of Glasgow and Edinburgh in Scotland.

Later generations have fondly referred to the men at the Philadelphia convention as Founding Fathers, but as a group they were surprisingly young to hold so many positions of leadership. A majority were under fifty (five were under thirty). The average age of the delegates was forty-three. The youngest was twenty-six-year-old Jonathan Dayton of New Jersey. Benjamin Franklin was the oldest at eighty-one. George Washington was fifty-five.

Thomas Jefferson, the author of the Declaration of Independence, did not attend the Constitutional Convention. At the time of this meeting he was in Paris, serving as the American minister to France.

The first to arrive at the convention was James Madison, who richly deserved the title by which he is still known today—"Father of the Constitution." No one came to Philadelphia better prepared for the task of creating a new government that did this scholarly young statesman from Virginia. Madison had spent the previous winter poring over boxes of books that Jefferson had sent him from Paris: volumes by Voltaire, Diderot, Necker, and many other political philosophers. He read everything he could find on political theories and on the history of governments from the time of the ancient Greeks to eighteenth-century Europe.

Although generally shy and soft-spoken, Madison was an impressive speaker and contributed more ideas to the formation of the Constitution (and later to the Bill of Rights) than did any other delegate. "He blends together the profound politician with the scholar," observed William Pierce, a delegate from Georgia. "In the management of every great question he evidently took the lead in the convention," Pierce continued. "From a spirit of industry and application which he possesses in a most eminent degree, he always comes forward the best informed man on any point in debate."

Madison was indeed a vocal member of the convention, taking part in its debates 161 times. He also provided the most extensive eyewitness account of the convention's proceedings. Madison kept a daily journal in which he meticulously recorded virtually everything that occurred during the four long months of meetings. Since newspaper reporters were barred from the convention hall, Madison's journal, which was made public in 1840 (four years after his death), proved to be a treasure house for historians who needed to learn all that had happened at Philadelphia in that crucial summer of 1787.

How was it possible for Madison to be such an active participant at all of the sessions, and also their chief recorder? Later he admitted that this was both difficult and strenuous, but Madison realized that one of history's most monumental dramas was unfolding before his eyes, and he vowed to capture all of it for posterity.

"I chose a seat in front of the presiding member," Madison explained, "with the other members on my right hand and left hand. In this favorable position for hearing all that passed I noted in terms legible and abbreviations and marks intelligible to myself what was read from the Chair or spoken by the members. . . . I was enabled to write out my daily notes during the session or within a few finishing days after its close. . . . It happened also that I was not absent a single day, nor more than a casual fraction of an hour in any day, so that I could not have lost a single speech, unless a very short one."

While Madison was thrilled to be at the convention, his fellow Virginian George Washington was very reluctant to attend the conference. At the conclusion of the Revolutionary War he had retired to his plantation at Mount Vernon and announced that his long years of public service had finally ended. Washington had declined an invitation to the Annapolis convention and had good reasons for not wanting to lead Virginia's delegation to Philadelphia. He was not feeling well; his rheumatism had gotten so painful that at times he could not lift his arm as high as his head. His elderly mother and sister, who lived nearby, were both very ill and often needed help. Also, Washington hesitated to leave his plantation because it needed his attention; there were repairs to be made and bills to be paid. He owed it to himself and his family to attend to these matters.

There were political reasons, as well as family reasons, that could have kept Washington away from the convention. If the men at Philadelphia disobeyed the instructions from Congress to only revise the Articles of Confederation—which Washington felt they were likely to do—the convention would go beyond its legal limitations. What would the citizens think if Washington was involved in an illegal scheme? And what if the states refused to accept the actions of the convention? Washington would be greatly embarrassed, and his reputation might be severely damaged. Then, too, if he accepted appointment as a delegate to the convention, people might say he had broken his word to stay out of public service for the rest of his life. They might call him a hypocrite and claim he was using the convention to gain personal power in the new government.

So Washington preferred to remain a gentleman farmer at Mount Vernon and let others argue at Philadelphia about the future course of the nation. But during March 1787 he received a flood of letters urging him to attend the convention. When Washington was told by wartime comrades that his participation might make the difference between the success and failure of the meeting, the loyal old soldier could resist no longer. On March 28 he wrote Governor Edmund Randolph that he would join the Virginia delegation at Philadelphia.

Shortly after Washington reached Philadelphia, he called on Benjamin Franklin, who as the president (governor) of Pennsylvania was the host of the convention. Franklin, next to Washington, was the best-known and most respected American at home and abroad. He had acquired widespread fame as a statesman, a scholar and writer, and a scientist-inventor. But at eighty-one he was ill from gout and what his doctors called "the stone." Because his ailments made walking and riding in a carriage very uncomfortable, Franklin had to be carried the short distance from his house to the convention hall in a sedan chair borne by four prisoners from the Walnut Street jail. Even though he was not strong enough to attend all the sessions, Franklin was known to be a faithful supporter of a strong central government, and his enormous prestige carried much weight.

Alexander Hamilton, on the other hand, sadly discovered that his influence at the convention would be very limited. Although the brilliant thirty-two-year-old lawyer stood in the forefront among those who wanted a more powerful union, the other two New York delegates, Robert Yates and John Lansing, Jr., were fervent believers in state sovereignty. Since each state had only one vote in the convention, Hamilton was outvoted two to one whenever New York cast its ballot on major issues. As the convention progressed, Yates and Lansing realized that their ideas would not prevail, so they packed

Benjamin Franklin was the oldest delegate at the Constitutional Convention, and his wit often reduced tensions when tempers flared.

their bags and left for home. But Hamilton's position was not helped much by their departure. The convention had assigned each state a quorum, which was the number of delegates from that state who must be present in order for the state to vote. New York's quorum was two delegates, so when Hamilton became his state's lone representative, New York lost its vote.

The delegate who made the most speeches at the convention was Gouverneur Morris of Pennsylvania. Morris was a fun-loving, high-living bachelor who had a keen eye for pretty women and fast horses. Having lost a leg in a carriage accident, he stomped about on a wooden peg. Morris addressed the convention 173 times, often lacing his gracefully phrased remarks with touches of humor. Fellow delegate William Pierce wrote, "[Morris] winds through all the mazes of rhetoric, and . . . charms, captivates, and leads away the senses of all who hear him."

The next most talkative delegate, delivering 168 speeches, was James Wilson, also from Pennsylvania. Wilson was a signer of the Declaration of Independence, a member of the Continental Congress, and one of the ablest lawyers in the country. Speaking with a Scottish accent (he had come to America from Scotland twenty years earlier), time and time again Wilson brilliantly pleaded the case of the nationalists. Textbooks usually give him scant attention, but Wilson was probably the unsung hero of the Philadelphia convention.

Other distinguished Americans were in the cast of characters at the convention. Robert Morris (no relation to Gouverneur Morris), the financial wizard who almost singlehandedly kept the American economy afloat during the Revolutionary War, was a representative from Pennsylvania. South Carolina sent its wartime governor, John Rutledge, and the two Pinckneys, Charles and his cousin Charles Cotesworth. From Delaware came John Dickinson, a member of the Second Continental Congress who had refused to sign the Declaration of Independence. Earlier Dickinson had been governor of Pennsylvania, and after moving to Delaware, this capable man was elected governor of that state.

Gouverneur Morris of Pennsylvania made the most speeches at the Constitutional Convention and played a major role in writing the Constitution.

James Wilson, who had come to America from Scotland, was one of the principal architects of the Constitution.

The New Jersey delegation included Governor William Livingston and William Paterson, the state's former attorney general, who became the chief spokesman at the convention for the cause of the small states. Two influential representatives from Connecticut were a wily ex-shoemaker, Roger Sherman, and Oliver Ellsworth, a judge of the state supreme court. The delegates from Massachusetts who played large roles at the convention were Rufus King, a member of the Continental Congress, and longtime politician Elbridge Gerry, who had signed both the Declaration of Independence and the Articles of Confederation. Besides Madison and Washington, two other prominent Virginians at the convention were Governor Edmund Randolph and George Mason, Washington's fox-hunting planter neighbor, who authored his state's Bill of Rights.

An interesting situation developed in New Hampshire. That state had voted to send delegates to the convention, but it did not have the funds to pay their travel expenses. One of the delegates was John Langdon, who previously had served as president (governor) of New Hampshire. A wealthy Portsmouth merchant, Langdon favored a stronger central government that would establish forceful regulations for commerce and trade. So he came to the rescue of his home state and supplied the travel money out of his own pocket for himself and the other New Hampshire delegate, Nicholas Gilman.

The most outspoken delegate from Maryland was Luther Martin, the state attorney general. Martin's first loyalty was to his state, and he argued vehemently against the formation of a strong national government until he left the convention in disgust on September 4.

Most of the influential Americans who opposed a stronger union refused to attend the Philadelphia convention. Patrick Henry, suspicious of the convention's anti-Confederation bias, said that he "smelled a rat" and would have nothing to do with the "illegal" meeting. Another Virginian, Richard Henry Lee, who had introduced the resolution of independence in the Continental Congress in 1776, felt the same way. So did patriots Sam Adams and John Hancock of Massachusetts.

Thomas Jefferson, on the other hand, might have attended the convention (although he did not agree with all the actions it took), if at that time he had not been the American minister to Paris. John Adams would have been a likely delegate, but in the summer of 1787 he was our minister to London.

The delegates met in the East Room of the Philadelphia State House, the same room in which the Continental Congress had held its sessions and in which the Declaration of Independence had been signed. The room, about forty feet square, was painted blue-gray. It had high windows on two sides. Whether their blinds were open or shut, the weather was oppressively hot and humid inside the meeting room, and the delegates frequently had to wipe perspiration from their faces and necks.

It was a noisy room, too. Countless large flies buzzed about, and speakers had to interrupt their remarks to swat at those that lit on their bodies. Street noises outside were distracting. The delegates had to persuade city officials to cover the street in front of the State House with a layer of gravel that lessened the rumble of carriages and the clippity-clop of horses' hooves.

The delegates sat three or four together at square tables covered with green baize (a thick woolen cloth). On the tables were inkwells and long quill pens. Against one paneled wall, on a dais (low platform) between two fireplaces, was the presiding officer's chair with a sun carved on its back.

One of the first steps taken at the convention's opening session surprised no one. Robert Morris nominated George Washington to serve as president, and Washington was elected unanimously. The beloved general was formally escorted to the chair on the dais, where he would preside for the next four months with great dignity.

Among the rules of procedure that the convention adopted, one was especially important. The delegates agreed to maintain complete secrecy about their deliberations. This meant that neither newspaper reporters nor spectators would be allowed in the convention hall. It also meant that no delegate could discuss with any outsider what the members were doing in their sessions.

The Constitution was created and debated in the Assembly Room of Independence Hall.

The convention members invoked this rule partly because they wanted to be free to change their minds on certain issues without being concerned about how the public would react to these changes. They also did not want to be pressured by various groups or factions that had their own axes to grind. Madison wrote to Jefferson that secrecy was needed "to secure unbiased discussion within doors and to prevent misconceptions and misconstructions without."

Some delegates were optimistic about the exciting challenge that lay ahead. "After the lapse of six thousand years since the creation of the world," James Wilson observed, "America now presents the first instance of a people assembled to weigh deliberately and calmly and to decide leisurely and peaceably upon the form of government by which they will bind themselves and their posterity."

Still, Wilson's lofty goal seemed far out of reach to many experienced politicians at the convention. Would it not be better, they argued, simply to make some piecemeal revisions to prop up the Articles of Confederation, as Congress had intended them to do? If they stopped at this, they could count on the support of the overwhelming majority of American citizens. As the old adage said, wasn't half a loaf better than no loaf at all?

Several delegates expressed these doubts to Washington before the convention's first session. But the proud old general had not forsaken his duties and comforts at Mount Vernon to preside over a convention that would be content with halfway measures and partial reforms. "If to please the people we offer what we ourselves disapprove," Washington asked the doubters, "how can we afterwards defend our work? Let us raise a standard to which the wise and honest can repair. The event is in the hand of God."

George Washington, the most beloved American of his day, presided over the Constitutional Convention.

5

Two Conflicting Plans

The nationalists came to Philadelphia prepared to seize the initiative. On May 29, the day the convention began, Edmund Randolph of Virginia introduced fifteen resolutions for the delegates to consider. These resolutions, drafted largely by Madison, were known as the Virginia Plan.

This plan boldly called for a new national government with broad powers. It would be composed of three branches—legislative, executive, and judicial. The new legislature (Congress) would consist of two houses instead of the one-house legislature under the Articles of Confederation. Representation in both houses was to be based upon either each state's population or the amount of money that the state contributed to the support of the central government.

The members of the lower house (the House of Representatives) were to be elected by the people, and those of the upper house (the Senate) were to be chosen by the lower house from candidates nominated by the state legislatures. Congress was to be given all the powers it held under the Articles of Confederation. In addition, it would have the power to make laws in all cases where the states either were "incompetent" or would interrupt "the harmony of the

United States." Furthermore, Congress could veto any state
law in conflict with national law and had the power to force a
state to obey all congressional acts.

The Virginia Plan said that the "national executive"
would be chosen by Congress and given the authority to execute the national laws. The judges who were to make up the
"national judiciary" would be selected by Congress, too. Together, the "national executive" and a convenient number of
the "national judiciary" would compose a "council of revision" with the power to veto acts of Congress.

Another provision of the Virginia Plan would guarantee
each state a republican form of government, thereby prevent-
ing the rise of a dictator or the overthrow of a state government by armed insurgents, such as those in Shays' Rebellion.
Also, all state officers had to take an oath to support the
United States.

The Virginia Plan called for a dual system of government—eventually to be known as a federal system—which
was unheard of in 1787. It did not suggest that the states be
stripped of all their powers and become mere branches of the
national government. Instead, it permitted both the national
government and the state governments to exercise authority
over the people, each within separate, specified areas. Randolph explained that the Virginia Plan "only [meant] to give
the national government power to defend and protect itself—
to take, therefore, from the respective legislatures of states no
more sovereignty than [was] competent to this end."

When Randolph finished speaking, the convention turned
itself into a Committee of the Whole. This was an old British
parliamentary device that allowed delegates to debate at
length and take informal votes that would not bind them to
vote the same way when official votes were cast later. Whenever the convention was meeting as a Committee of the
Whole, Washington stepped down from the platform and
joined the rest of the Virginia delegation on the floor.

Hardly had debate on the Virginia Plan begun when Randolph moved, "A *national* Government ought to be estab-

lished consisting of a *supreme* Legislative, Executive, and Judiciary." Gouverneur Morris seconded the proposal, warning, "We had better take a *supreme* government now than a despot twenty years hence—for come he must."

There was surprisingly little opposition to Randolph's motion. The delegates were familiar with three-branch governments in their states, and many of them believed that a glaring weakness of the Articles of Confederation was that it had no effective executive and judicial branches. Randolph's proposition was adopted with only Connecticut opposed and New York divided. At that moment the die was cast; the majority of delegates were determined to write a constitution for a supreme national government rather than a revision of the Confederation government.

On many important details the delegates sharply disagreed. Some of them objected to the resolution that the lower house of the legislature ought to be elected by the people. Roger Sherman of Connecticut maintained that the people should have "as little to do as may be about the government." Believing that ordinary citizens could not make intelligent, informed decisions, Sherman wanted the state legislatures to elect members of the House of Representatives. Elbridge Gerry of Massachusetts and Charles Pinckney of South Carolina agreed. Pinckney believed that "the people were less fit judges."

To this argument George Mason of Virginia sternly replied, "We ought to attend the rights of every class of people." He reminded the convention that the will of the people was "the grand depository [storehouse] of the democratic principles of the government." And Pennsylvania's James Wilson, his steel spectacles hooked to his wig, observed in his Scottish brogue that "no government could long subsist without the confidence of the people."

When the vote was taken, the motion for election by the people carried. But this issue was not really settled then. Like so many other debatable questions, it would be brought up again and again in future sessions.

Governor Edmund Randolph of Virginia introduced the Virginia Plan, which called for a national government with powers divided among the legislative, executive, and judicial branches.

While the Virginia Plan called for a "national executive," it gave no details about how this branch of the government should be set up. So the delegates came forth with a wide variety of proposals. Alexander Hamilton, who actually preferred a constitutional monarch, called for a president elected for life. At the opposite extreme, Edmund Randolph was so fearful that "one-man rule" would turn into a monarchy or dictatorship that he even opposed the idea of a single executive. Randolph wanted the executive power divided among three persons. So did George Mason, who suggested that the three presidents include one from the South, one from the North, and one from the Middle States. Even wise old Dr. Franklin had his doubts about a single president. He warned that though the first man at the helm would be a good one (George Washington, he presumed), "who could say what manner of leader might come after?"

Most of the delegates, however, agreed that there should be only one president. They sided with James Wilson, who predicted that there would be "nothing but uncontrolled, continued and violent animosities" among three presidents. But how long should the president serve? Rufus King of Massachusetts suggested a twenty-year term, since this was the average length of the rule of kings. Wilson said this was much too long and suggested a three-year term of office with reelection possible. Charles Pinckney offered a compromise: a seven-year term without the possibility of reelection. His suggestion carried by a five-to-four vote, with Massachusetts divided. In the end, however, the convention decided that there should be a single executive elected to a four-year term. The executive would be eligible for reelection.

For several weeks the delegates debated various parts of the Virginia Plan. Often they would tentatively accept an idea, such as the single seven-year term for the president, and then later reverse their position. What went on in their secret sessions kept the public guessing. What were the sweaty delegates, confronted by the sweltering heat, the multitude of droning flies, and the endless arguments, doing to the government behind closed doors in the Philadelphia State House?

Rumors abounded, some with merit, others ridiculous. One persistent rumor was that the convention planned to establish a monarchy and invite the bishop of Osnaburgh, the second son of George III, to take the American throne.

Little did the public know that the most controversial part of the Virginia Plan concerned the number of votes each state would have in the national legislature. This hot issue almost brought some of the delegates to blows! Under the Articles of Confederation each state was equal to every other state in the one-house Congress because each state had only one vote. But the Virginia Plan proposed a two-house Congress in which each state would have a different number of votes (and members), the number to be based on its population or its tax contributions to the central government. Supporters of this concept argued that Congress should represent the people, not the states, and that the states with more people should have more votes.

This proposal was angrily opposed by delegates from the smaller states. They felt the large states would completely dominate both houses of Congress. Luther Martin of Maryland figured that the three most populous states—Virginia, Pennsylvania, and Massachusetts—would have nearly half the seats in both the Senate and the House of Representatives. Such an arrangement, Martin grumbled, meant "a system of slavery which bound hand and foot ten states of the Union at the mercy of the other three."

John Dickinson of tiny Delaware asserted that his state's instructions were to leave the convention if the one-state, one-vote principle were tampered with. "We would rather submit to a foreign power," growled Dickinson, "than submit to be deprived of an equality of suffrage [votes] in both branches of the legislature, and thereby be thrown under the domination of the large states." William Paterson of New Jersey, a wisp of a man only five feet two inches tall, rose from his seat and flatly announced that New Jersey would "never confederate" on the basis suggested in the Virginia Plan, for "she would be swallowed up." He said his state would "rather submit to a monarch, to a despot, than to such a fate."

But the defenders of the Virginia Plan, also known as the large-state plan, refused to give in to the demands of the representatives from the small states. Benjamin Franklin scolded the small-state delegations for their inflexible attitude. "We are sent here to consult, not to contend with each other," Franklin said crisply, "and declarations of a fixed opinion . . . neither enlighten nor convince us." Franklin thought that the opponents of congressional representation based on population were unduly concerned about its effects. "I do not at present see what advantage the greater states could propose to themselves by swallowing the smaller, and therefore do not apprehend they would attempt it."

The first time that the Committee of the Whole voted on whether representation in both houses should be based on population, the measure carried, six states to five. But the vote was extremely close, and the small-state delegations vowed they would not surrender. Connecticut's Roger Sherman then stepped into the fray as a peacemaker. Let the large states have what they wanted in the House of Representatives, Sherman suggested, by basing its membership on population. Then let the small states have what they wanted in the Senate by giving each state an equal number of votes in that house. Some delegates felt this was a fair arrangement, but when it was first voted upon, Sherman's compromise did not have enough support to be adopted.

Now the small-state delegations abandoned their defensive tactics and counterattacked. They presented an alternate plan to the convention that included the principles they championed. Because it was introduced by William Paterson of New Jersey, the small-state plan came to be called the New Jersey Plan.

Paterson said that this plan was essentially a revision of the Articles of Confederation. He reminded the delegates that they had strayed far from the stated purpose of the convention and had suggested sweeping changes in the central government that the people would probably reject. On the other hand, the New Jersey Plan "accorded first with the powers of the Convention," Paterson explained, "and second with the sentiments of the people. . . . Our object is not such a Government as may be best in itself, but such a one as our constituents have authorized us to prepare and as they will approve."

There were two major ways in which the New Jersey Plan differed from the Virginia Plan. First, it called for a one-house legislature that would have an equal number of members from every state. Second, it provided for an executive council (instead of a single president) that would be elected by the legislature. This plural executive would have the power to veto bills but not the authority to appoint national judges.

Under the New Jersey Plan, Congress was to control foreign and interstate commerce and have the power to tax, coin money, and admit new states. The laws of the national legislature were to be supreme, and the legislatures of the states could not pass bills that conflicted with national laws or with treaties entered into by the central government.

In spite of what Paterson said, the New Jersey Plan provided for much more than a simple revision of the Articles of Confederation, and, since the Articles insisted that every amendment must have the unanimous approval of all the states, it is unlikely that Paterson's proposals would have been acceptable to every state.

Madison and Wilson assailed the New Jersey Plan for not providing a two-house legislature with membership in both houses based on population. They argued that this plan continued state sovereignty, while the Virginia Plan made the will of the people supreme.

On June 19 the convention voted on the two conflicting plans: seven states preferred the Virginia Plan, three states chose the New Jersey Plan, and one state was divided. But the small states still would not give up the fight. In fact, the debate grew more intense, and tempers reached the boiling point. Gunning Bradford, Jr., of Delaware, his face flushed with anger, shouted at the delegates from the large states, "I do not, gentlemen, trust you!" Then he threatened that his state not only would withdraw from the union but would seek an alliance with one of the "foreign powers" in Europe!

William Paterson presented the New Jersey Plan that was favored by delegates from the small states because it proposed equal representation in a one-house congress.

Feelings ran so high on the convention floor that Benjamin Franklin, generally not known as a religious man, begged the delegates to have a minister open each session with a prayer. The convention could not even agree on this request: Hamilton is said to have objected that the delegates did not need "foreign aid," and others pointed out that their group had no funds with which to hire a minister.

On July 2 the convention voted on whether the states would have equal representation in the Senate. The states split five to five, with Georgia divided. (The twelfth state was New Hampshire, but its delegation had not yet arrived in Philadelphia.)

A hopeless deadlock had occurred. Expressing the utter dejection of many delegates, Roger Sherman sadly observed that the convention had come to a "full stop." In desperation, the men grasped at a suggestion made by Charles Cotesworth Pinckney. He proposed that the convention form a "Grand Committee" composed of one member from each of the states. It would try to devise some compromise acceptable to both the large and the small states.

The convention appointed this Grand Committee. Then, since the Fourth of July was two days hence, it adjourned until after the holiday.

On Independence Day, 1787, Philadelphians celebrated merrily. Bells chimed, guns roared, and people drank the traditional thirteen toasts to the thirteen states. Some of the convention delegates, including George Washington, spent part of the holiday fishing. But the group known as the Grand Committee had hardly any time to observe the holiday. They spent a busy and fateful day trying to find the glue that would hold the convention together.

6

Compromises Pave the Way

On the morning of July 5 the Grand Committee presented its report to the convention. The compromise it offered was very similar to the one Roger Sherman had proposed earlier which the convention had turned down. However, the Grand Committee added a third provision to the two suggested by Sherman.

The first provision of the compromise said that in the House of Representatives each state would be allowed one representative for every forty thousand inhabitants. The second provision said each state would be allowed an equal number of members in the Senate. The new third provision said that bills for raising and spending money must start in the House of Representatives. This provision giving the House the sole power to originate money bills was a major concession to the larger states who would have the most members in the House.

These resolutions were hotly debated for the next ten days. They were finally adopted on July 16 by a five-to-four vote, with Massachusetts divided and New York not voting because the two of its three delegates who believed in state sovereignty had departed. This agreement, which later was called the Great Compromise, broke the logjam and cleared a path to further compromises.

Roger Sherman of Connecticut played a large role in bringing about the crucial compromise between the large and small states.

Since population would be the basis for allotting seats in the House of Representatives, the southern states naturally wanted their black slaves counted as part of their populations. On the other hand, direct taxes owed to the national government were to be levied on the basis of the population of each state, and southerners did not want their slaves included in this count. After much wrangling, the delegates agreed to another compromise: all "free persons" and "three-fifths of all other persons" would be counted in determining a state's representation in the House, as well as the taxes it owed. (The words "slaves" and "slavery" do not appear anywhere in the Constitution.)

This "three-fifths" compromise had resolved a serious question, but there were still other issues dividing the North and South. One was the power to regulate commerce. The chaotic conditions of commerce had been a major reason for holding the Philadelphia convention. The states north of the Potomac, which dominated shipping and were developing manufacturing, were anxious to give Congress the power to regulate commerce and pass navigation laws that would protect shipping from foreign competition. But the southern states were largely agricultural, and their planters feared that if Congress controlled commerce it would levy taxes on their farm exports and abolish the slave trade. So a third compromise was forged, which gave Congress the power to regulate commerce and to levy duties on imports, but forbade the national government to tax exports or to interfere with the importation of "persons" (slaves) until 1808.

Settling the differences between North and South did not mean that the convention's work was done. Numerous other provisions for the legislative, executive, and judicial branches of the new national government had to be made. Many of these provisions are discussed in Chapter 8.

Finally, on July 26 the convention created a Committee of Detail to organize all the decisions of the past two months into some sort of coherent, meaningful document. The convention then adjourned for ten days while the Committee of

Detail performed its difficult task. On August 6 the Committee of Detail presented a draft containing a preamble and twenty-three articles divided into forty-one sections. For the next month these articles were discussed, and some changes were made.

Then came the job of polishing the wording in the Constitution and putting it into final shape. A five-man Committee of Style was named, with William Johnson of Connecticut its chairman. The other committee members were Gouverneur Morris, Hamilton, Madison, and Rufus King of Massachusetts. The committee reduced the number of articles from twenty-three to seven. It also made a significant change in the preamble that reinforced the concept that the national government would be supreme. The original wording of the preamble began: "We, the people of the states of. . . ." (Then it named all the states.) The new preamble started: "We, the People of the United States, in order to form a more perfect union. . . ."

Gouverneur Morris took the leading role in the Committee of Style and was the chief author of the Constitution. When the document was offered to the convention on September 12, there were still some objections. George Mason and Elbridge Gerry were concerned that the Constitution had no bill of rights. They felt it was necessary to include in the supreme law of the land specific promises to protect the rights and liberties of the people. Roger Sherman disagreed, saying that since most state constitutions contained either a bill of rights or restrictions prohibiting the government from interfering with the citizens' liberties, there was no need to add a list of personal rights to the national Constitution. Gerry went ahead and moved that a bill of rights be included in the Constitution; Mason seconded the motion. When the measure was voted upon, not a single state cast its ballot in favor of adding a bill of rights. This proved to be an unfortunate mistake. But most delegates did not foresee that the lack of a bill of rights would, in several states, greatly handicap the campaign to ratify the Constitution.

The last alteration made in the Constitution was suggested by George Washington. Stepping down from the dais, he requested and obtained unanimous approval to change the number of people represented by each member of the House of Representatives from forty thousand to thirty thousand. This was the only speech Washington made at the convention.

On Monday, September 17, the convention met for the final time. The Constitution was ready to be signed, and Benjamin Franklin urged all of the delegates to put their signatures on it. Franklin was too frail to address the convention, so James Wilson read his remarks for him:

> Mr. President, I confess that there are several parts of this Constitution which I do not at present approve, but I am not sure that I shall never approve them. For having lived long, I have experienced many instances of being obliged by better information or fuller consideration, to change opinions even on important subjects which I once thought right but found to be otherwise. It is therefore that the older I grow, the more apt I am to doubt my own judgment and to pay more respect to the judgment of others. . . .
>
> I doubt too whether any other convention we can obtain may be able to make a better Constitution. For when you assemble a number of men to have the advantage of their joint wisdom, you inevitably assemble with those men all their prejudices, their passions, their errors of opinion, their local interests, and their selfish views. From such an assembly can a perfect production be assembled? It therefore astonishes me, sir, to find this system approaching so near to perfection as it does. . . . Thus, I consent, sir, to the Constitution because I expect no better, and because I am not sure, that it is not the best. . . .
>
> On the whole, sir, I cannot help expressing a wish that every member of the convention who may still have objections to it, would with me, on this occasion, doubt a little of his own fallibility—and to make manifest our unanimity, put his name to this instrument.

Delegates signed the Constitution on September 17, 1787.

These remarks were addressed to the forty-one delegates who were still present at the convention on its last day. The other fourteen had departed, some because they felt they had more pressing matters, and four—Robert Yates and John Lansing of New York, and Luther Martin and John Mercer of Maryland—because they opposed the Constitution. John Dickinson had been taken ill, but before he left, he gave a letter to George Read authorizing him to sign his name.

Of the forty-one delegates at the Philadelphia State House on this momentous occasion, three refused to put their signatures on the historic document. Ironically, Edmund Randolph of Virginia, the man who had introduced the Virginia Plan, now opposed adoption of the Constitution. He expressed the fear that the new government he had helped to create was too revolutionary for the citizens to accept, and he proposed that state conventions debate its provisions and offer amendments. Then a second convention would be called to consider the amendments offered by the states.

Fellow Virginian George Mason seconded Randolph's motion and declared that unless a second convention was provided for, he could not approve the Constitution. All the states voted no on Randolph's motion. Besides Randolph and Mason, Elbridge Gerry of Massachusetts was the other dissenter who would not sign the Constitution. Gerry objected to a number of its provisions, including some of those that gave Congress vast new powers.

As the thirty-eight delegates slowly filed forward to put their names at the bottom of the Constitution (and Dickinson's name in absentia), Benjamin Franklin made another of his shrewd observations. He said that often during the four long months of deliberations, he had looked at the sun carved on the back of Washington's chair "without being able to tell whether it was rising or setting. But now at length," the old smiling statesman declared, "I have the happiness to know that it is a rising and not a setting sun."

The nationalists at the convention had won a stunning victory. But the war was only half over. The decisive battle still

Although delegate Elbridge Gerry of Massachusetts refused to sign the Constitution, later he became vice-president of the United States.

lay ahead—to persuade the American people to adopt the Constitution. Nevertheless, the Founding Fathers had reason to be extremely proud of their historic accomplishment. They had managed to provide for a central government with ample powers that could function independently of the states. And in all areas outside the jurisdiction of the national government, the states retained powers to make their own laws.

Furthermore, the Founding Fathers, determined to prevent any tyranny, had wisely divided the powers of the national government among three branches: legislative, executive, and judicial.

7

The Struggle for Ratification

The Founding Fathers exercised shrewd judgment in devising the method used for ratifying the Constitution. To turn ratification over to the Confederation Congress would have been sheer folly; the congressmen could not have been expected to vote themselves out of their jobs. To submit the Constitution to the state legislatures would have been risky, too. Many state legislators were totally committed to the notion of state supremacy and would have emphatically rejected a document that put the interests of the nation above those of their states. So the Philadelphia convention turned directly to the people to make the fateful decision. As Madison said, the Constitution should be ratified "by the supreme authority of the people themselves."

Every state was to have a ratifying convention, with delegates to it elected by all the eligible voters in the state. While there was no assurance that the voters would select pro-Constitution delegates, this method offered a much better chance of success than laying the matter in the laps of entrenched state legislators.

Then came the slyest, but wisest, decision of all. Shortly before it completed the Constitution, the Philadelphia convention added this final article: "The ratification of the conventions of nine states shall be sufficient for the establishment of the Constitution" So only *nine* states, not all thirteen, needed to ratify the Constitution before it could go into effect and become the supreme law of the land. If the delegates had insisted on a unanimous vote of the states to ratify the Constitution, it would not have been adopted. Two states, Rhode Island and North Carolina, refused to ratify the Constitution until *after* the national government started, so if a unanimous vote had been required, the government would not have gone into effect in 1789, and the United States would not have become the nation it is today!

The stage was now set for one of the most hard-fought battles in American history. Those who favored ratification probably should have been called nationalists. But instead they called themselves Federalists, which was a clever political trick to impress the voters that the Constitution called for a federal system that divided the powers between the national and state governments. Their opponents became known as Antifederalists. The Federalists and Antifederalists were the embryos of the first two American political parties.

In general, the people who earned their living by some type of commerce—bankers, shipowners, small shopkeepers, large merchants, manufacturers, city artisans, and wealthy planters near navigable waters—tended to support the Constitution. So did many newspaper editors, lawyers, and doctors. The large class of small farmers, especially those in debt or those who lived in the backcountry, tended to oppose it. But there were many exceptions to these generalizations. For example, some of the large landholders in New York's rich Hudson Valley were avid Antifederalists. So were some of the wealthy southern plantation owners, like George Mason of Virginia. On the other hand, some groups of poor farmers in the backcountry favored the Constitution because they wanted a government strong enough to protect them from Indian raids.

The Federalists had the advantages of being better organized and supporting a definite, concrete proposal. The Antifederalists were not able to offer the country anything more

George Mason, who authored Virginia's Bill of Rights, fought against ratification of the Constitution, largely because it had no bill of rights.

promising than the continuation of the ineffectual Articles of Confederation or a second constitutional convention that would probably haggle for months about every resolution. Nevertheless, the Antifederalists had many objections to the Constitution. They were concerned because it lacked a bill of rights. They argued that the Constitution destroyed the sovereignty of the states and that the president would have the powers of a king. Antifederalists also charged that the new government would try to impose a state religion, burden the people with heavy new taxes, and forbid states to print their own paper money or collect duties on products that crossed their borders.

Just as the believers in a strong central government had proposed their Virginia Plan to the Philadelphia convention before the opposition could organize, they now seized the initiative in seeking speedy ratification. On September 28, less than two weeks after the Philadelphia convention ended, the Federalists in the Pennsylvania Assembly demanded that a meeting date be set for their state convention to ratify the Constitution. But before the date could be selected, the presiding officer explained that the Assembly could conduct no business because it was two persons short of having a quorum. Nineteen Antifederalist assemblymen had not answered the roll call because they were boycotting the meeting.

The Federalist members waited impatiently for their absent colleagues to return, but they had locked themselves in a house and refused to budge. When they still did not come out the next day, a gang of Federalist supporters went after them. (These were artisans and mechanics who wanted a strong government that could improve trade with Europe and increase the demand for their skills.) They smashed open the front door of the house where the Antifederalists were hiding. They grabbed two of the Antifederalist assemblymen and dragged them to the State House. Now there was a quorum. Quickly the Assembly voted, forty-five to two, to set the first Tuesday in November as election day for selecting delegates to the state convention.

Little Delaware, however, earned the honor of becoming the first state in the United States. On December 7, 1787, its convention voted unanimously to ratify the Constitution.

Then the action switched back to Pennsylvania, where the debate was fierce and prolonged. The chief issue was the absence of a bill of rights. Day after day James Wilson pleaded for ratification, tirelessly, intelligently, and at last successfully. By a vote of forty-three to twenty-three the Pennsylvania convention finally accepted the Constitution. Federalists throughout the state celebrated their victory. At a ratification party in the little town of Carlisle, Wilson was scheduled to be the main speaker. After his opening remarks, this loyal champion of the Constitution was suddenly attacked by a mob of Antifederalists armed with clubs. They pulled him from the platform, threw him to the ground, and began beating him mercilessly. Later it was said that he would have been killed had not an old soldier fallen on his body and shielded Wilson from some of the blows.

The next two state conventions, in New Jersey and Georgia, ratified the Constitution unanimously. In Connecticut the cause of ratification was argued adroitly by two staunch defenders, Roger Sherman and Oliver Ellsworth. Again the question of a bill of rights came to the fore. Ellsworth sought to answer Antifederalist objections with a touch of humor. Admitting that freedom of speech was not included in the Constitution, he said, "Nor is liberty of conscience, or of matrimony, or of burial of the dead, but it is enough that Congress has no power to prohibit either, and can have no temptation." Sherman and Ellsworth were able to steer ratification through the Connecticut convention by a three-to-one margin.

Massachusetts, where the rural resentments that had sparked Shays' Rebellion still smoldered, presented a more difficult challenge. Of the huge convention of 355 delegates that met in January 1788, the majority were Antifederalists, and twenty-nine had been followers of Shays. Here, when the absence of a bill of rights was brought up again, the Federalists used a different strategy. This time they suggested that the delegates ratify the Constitution and then add a series of recommended amendments that the first Congress would consider.

John Hancock was the popular governor of Massachusetts, and the Federalists sought his support. But even though he was president of the ratification convention, Hancock, who had an attack of gout, retreated to his mansion until he could determine which way the political wind would blow. The Federalists appealed to Hancock's large ego by proposing that he present the recommended amendments to the convention as if they were his creation. Also, some Federalists may have whispered to the Massachusetts governor that if—as seemed likely—Virginia failed to ratify, then George Washington would not be available for the presidency. Should that happen, Hancock could become the nation's first president. All this flattery accomplished its purpose. Hancock came out in favor of the Constitution, and the Massachusetts convention ratified it by a vote of 187 to 168.

Maryland and South Carolina adopted the Constitution by large margins. Now a yes vote had been recorded in eight states—one short of the necessary nine.

Nevertheless, supporters of the Constitution knew that the rest of the battle was all uphill. Rhode Island and North Carolina almost certainly would oppose the Constitution. New Hampshire was on the fence and could go either way. And New York and Virginia posed special problems. Both states had influential, articulate Antifederalists who would wage savage attacks against the new form of government. If either state rejected the Constitution, the new United States would be badly crippled. Virginia, the home of Washington, Jefferson, and Madison, was the most populous state, and the Union would appear weak without it. If New York said no, the nation would be bisected, with New England separated from the states to its south.

In Virginia the Antifederalists rolled out their biggest guns—Patrick Henry, George Mason, and Richard Henry Lee—to attack the Constitution. Henry, the most eloquent speaker of his time, lashed out with all of his oratorical fury at the document conceived by the Philadelphia convention he had refused to attend. "Four-fifths of our inhabitants are opposed to the new scheme of government," he shouted at the ratifying convention assembled at Richmond. Twisting his ill-fitting brown wig around his head and at times even waving it

When Governor John Hancock of Massachusetts finally decided to support the Constitution, he helped it win ratification in his state's convention.

aloft to emphasize a point, Henry appealed by turns to the poor dirt farmers, the rich slaveowners, the debtors who longed for the state presses to print more paper money, and those who feared the national government would support an established church.

At the heart of Henry's opposition and that of the other Virginia Antifederalists was the gnawing fear that a Constitution devoid of a bill of rights would trample to death their personal liberties. "It is said eight states have adopted this plan," Henry stated. "I declare that if twelve states and a half had adopted it, I would with manly firmness, and in spite of an erring world, reject it. . . . Liberty, greatest of all earthly blessings—give us that precious jewel, and you may take everything else!"

The Virginia Antifederalists wanted their convention to introduce a bill of rights, and they urged that the adoption of the Constitution be postponed until all the states had accepted these new amendments. Federalists replied that this was neither logical nor practical. Eight states already had ratified the document; under the Antifederalists' plan all of them would have to hold new conventions and go through the whole business of ratifying the Constitution again. Although the Virginia Federalists would not yield on the question of adding a bill of rights then and there, they did have to make a major concession to their opponents in order to steer the Constitution successfully through their state convention. Madison and the other nationalists had to promise that one of the first acts of the new Congress would be to propose a series of constitutional amendments embracing a bill of rights.

Madison's promise greatly helped the Federalist cause in Virginia. So did the reassuring knowledge that George Washington, the favorite son of Virginia, stood unflinchingly behind the Constitution (even though he was not present at the ratification convention). The Federalists were aided, too, by the surprise announcement that Edmund Randolph had joined their ranks. At Philadelphia he had refused to sign the Constitution, but, probably due to the skillful persuasion of Madison, he had changed his mind. With his customary flair for the dramatic, Randolph rose from his seat and declared that the world looked upon Americans "as little wanton bees, who had played for liberty, but had no sufficient solidity or wisdom" to keep it. Pointing to his arm, he proclaimed passionately, "I would assent to the lopping of this limb before I assent to the dissolution of the Union."

The Richmond convention was interrupted by a startling piece of news. On June 21 New Hampshire became the ninth state to ratify the Constitution. Regardless of what Virginia did, the Confederation Congress was dead. The new United States was born!

Four days later Virginia ratified the Constitution, eighty-nine delegates voting for it and seventy-nine against. Now only three states were still to be heard from.

When the sixty-five delegates had assembled for the New York convention at Poughkeepsie on June 17, 1788, there was little reason to believe that New York would accept the Constitution. Governor George Clinton, the outspoken leader of the Antifederalists, figured that he had at least two-thirds of the delegates on his side. The strategy of the New York Antifederalists was to demand a second national convention that would strip away most of the powers given to the central government at the Philadelphia convention. Clinton and his followers then could gleefully watch the follow-up convention tear the Constitution to shreds.

But Clinton had not reckoned with the tenacity and political cunning of his chief foe, Alexander Hamilton. This zealous champion of the Constitution decided to play a waiting game for two reasons: he wanted to wear down the resistance of the Antifederalists, and he hoped to postpone a decision in New York until after both New Hampshire and Virginia took their stands. (The New York convention lasted forty-one days.)

Hamilton's cause was helped by four New York newspapers that had printed in the fall of 1787 and the spring of 1788 a series of eighty-five letters that defended the Constitution and explained how it worked. All of the letters were signed "Publius" (the name of a Roman leader who had established a stable government). In May 1788 the letters were published in a book titled *The Federalist*. The real authors of these letters were Hamilton, Madison, and John Jay, a New Yorker who had been president of the Continental Congress. Hamilton wrote more than half of them. While it is doubtful that *The Federalist* had much influence on the delegates at Poughkeepsie, these essays remain the most brilliant and penetrating commentary ever written on the Constitution and are still widely read today.

Rumors began circulating in Poughkeepsie that if the New York convention refused to ratify, New York City might secede from the state, hold its own convention, and join the Union. This jolted the Antifederalists. So did the news that both New Hampshire and Virginia had voted yes. Recognizing that the opposition was wavering, Hamilton mounted the platform and in a scholarly manner pleaded the case for the Constitution. Section by section he dissected the document, attempting to show the Antifederalists that their fears were unwarranted. Some of the enemy came over to his side, and on July 26 the New York convention voted to ratify the Constitution by a razor-thin margin of thirty to twenty-seven.

Last-ditch dissent developed in the two remaining states. North Carolina held its convention in July 1888. Here one major issue was cheap paper money printed by the state government versus a single sound currency produced by the national government. There were also demands by Baptists and Presbyterians that their religious freedom be guaranteed, and many delegates added their voices to the swelling clamor for a bill of rights. On August 2 the Antifederalists won their first clear-cut victory. North Carolina rejected the Constitution by a whopping vote of 184 to 84.

Rhode Island, which had refused to send any delegates to the Constitutional Convention, did not even summon a ratifying convention. Instead, the Rhode Island legislature, dominated by debtor farmers, submitted the Constitution to town meetings. There it was soundly defeated by a vote of 2,708 to 237, but many Federalists, realizing they were in the minority, boycotted the meetings and refused to vote.

The new Union could survive without North Carolina and Rhode Island. The Constitution went into effect on March 4, 1789, and the nation's first capital was New York City. Soon afterward George Washington, the unanimous choice of the electoral college to be the first president, started the long, hard carriage ride from Mount Vernon to the capital city. At almost every town and village along the way he was greeted by jubilant crowds, cheering wildly and waving banners or tossing flower petals in the path of America's indispensable leader.

On the balcony of Federal Hall, at the corner of Wall and Broad streets, Washington was inaugurated on April 30. He was president of eleven United States—stubborn Rhode Island and North Carolina were, in effect, foreign countries.

Finally, in November 1789, North Carolina held a second convention, and its delegates, deciding their state could not exist safely and prosperously apart from the Union, ratified

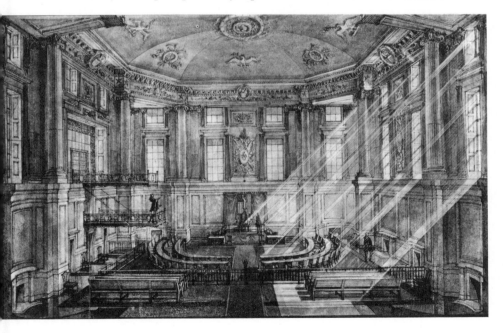

The first Congress met in Federal Hall in New York City.

The presidential inauguration of George Washington was held at Federal Hall.

the Constitution. Rhode Island held out longer. Not until May 1790, after the Senate had passed a bill ending trade between the United States and Rhode Island, did the smallest state join the Union. Even during the last gasps of their long struggle, the Antifederalists did not give up readily—Rhode Island accepted the Constitution by a vote of thirty-four to thirty-two.

Summing up the enormous advantages reaped by Americans under the Constitution, Dr. Benjamin Rush, the notable Philadelphia physician-statesman, wrote to John Adams, "[The Constitution] has a thousand . . . things to recommend it. It makes us a nation. It rescues us from anarchy and slavery. It revives agriculture and commerce. It checks moral and political iniquity. In a word, it makes a man both willing to *live* and to *die*. To *live*, because it opens to him fair prospects of great public and private happiness. To *die*, because it ensures peace, order, safety, and prosperity to his children."

PART THREE

OUR LIVING CONSTITUTION

8

The Three
Branches of Government

THE LEGISLATIVE BRANCH

The two-house Congress under the Constitution is similar in some respects to the British system, in which Parliament is divided into a House of Commons and a House of Lords. The House of Representatives was intended to resemble Commons and be more democratic, while the Senate was originally designed to resemble the House of Lords in being somewhat removed from popular control.

Some of the delegates to the Constitutional Convention wanted yearly elections for members of the House of Representatives. Gerry said that one-year terms were "the only defense against tyranny." But members of the lower house would have had to spend a large amount of time running for reelection. Madison proposed three-year terms, but the convention compromised and settled on a term of two years.

The delegates at Philadelphia were even more divided on matters relating to the Senate. Hamilton viewed the Senate as an aristocratic body and felt senators should be appointed to terms for life (like the members of the House of Lords). The most democratic delegates thought a four-year term was best. But the convention first voted for a seven-year term and later changed this to a six-year term, with one-third of the senators to be elected every two years.

Charlotte County Free Library
Charlotte Court House, Va.

31861

Another question was who should elect the senators. Should they be elected by the House from persons nominated by the state legislatures, as the Virginia Plan proposed? Most of the delegates did not like this idea. They felt it gave too much power to the House, and, as Gouverneur Morris observed, the Senate should act as a guardian to "check the . . . changeableness and excesses" of the lower house. Madison and Wilson wanted the people to elect the Senate as well as the House, but many delegates were against giving the people this much power. So it was finally decided to have the senators elected by their state legislatures, and this practice continued until the Seventeenth Amendment in 1913 allowed the people to vote directly for senators.

Some delegates at the Constitutional Convention wanted the states to pay the salaries of the members of Congress, but others disagreed. Hamilton said that this would make the legislators "the mere agents and advocates of state interests and views." Nevertheless, the report of the Committee of Detail provided that the pay of senators and representatives should be "ascertained and paid" by the states. But the convention later rejected this recommendation and on August 14, 1787, voted, nine to two, to pay members out of the national treasury. The delegates also argued about who should decide the amount to be paid to members of Congress. Oliver Ellsworth thought a flat rate of five dollars a day would be fair. The convention, however, decided to let Congress have the full authority to fix its own pay by law.

The Constitution gives a few separate special powers to each house of Congress. The House has the sole power to originate bills that involve raising and spending money (which was part of the Great Compromise). The Senate has the sole power to accept or reject persons the president has appointed to executive and judicial offices. Also, the Senate must ratify a treaty by at least a two-thirds vote before it can go into operation.

The House of Representatives has the right to impeach (charge with wrongdoing) members of the executive and judicial departments for "treason, bribery, or other high crimes and misdemeanors." The Senate acts as a court to try impeachment cases brought by the House, and a two-thirds vote of the senators is required to find the defendant guilty.

All of the bills offered in Congress must be passed in identical language by both houses to become effective. The powers of Congress are enormous but not unlimited. As stated in the Constitution, they include the power to lay and collect taxes; provide for the common defense and general welfare; borrow, coin, and regulate the value of money; regulate commerce; admit new states to the Union; establish post offices; declare war; raise and support armies; establish national courts in addition to the Supreme Court; and legislate for the District of Columbia.

The section of the Constitution listing the powers of Congress ends with one that has been especially important to generations that followed the Founding Fathers. It gives Congress the power "to make all laws which shall be necessary and proper for carrying into execution all the foregoing [previously listed] powers" This is the famous "elastic clause" that permits Congress to make all laws "necessary and proper" for putting into effect its stated powers. The Founding Fathers wisely realized they could not foresee the future and specify all the powers that Congress someday might need to deal with the changing problems of a growing country. For example, they knew nothing about airplanes or atomic weapons. But, by applying the "elastic clause," Congress in the twentieth century has been able to spend the money for planes and bombs that are needed to "provide for the common defense."

THE EXECUTIVE BRANCH

Our country came within a whisker of having a president chosen by Congress for one term of seven years! This was the prevailing idea in the Philadelphia Convention almost until it adjourned.

No branch of the national government gave the Founding Fathers more difficulty than the executive branch. They knew that a strong president was needed, but they also had to consider the widespread fear that the president could turn into a tyrant. Americans remembered only too well their struggles against overbearing royal governors in colonial times and their hatred of the oppressive George III during the Revolutionary War.

So the Constitution makers had to treat with extreme caution all questions related to the presidency—the length of the executive's term, the manner of election, and the powers that would be vested in this individual. The decision to give the president a four-year term was a difficult one to reach. But the way the chief executive would be selected was an even thornier issue; sixty ballots were taken before the delegates finally reached an agreement.

The delegates rejected the resolution in the Virginia Plan that the executive be elected by the legislature because it would make the president a powerless puppet of Congress. A few of the Founding Fathers wanted the president elected by the people, but this idea was turned down for a number of reasons. Some of the people were illiterate or had only a slight education. Large numbers of them were uninformed about issues and candidates. In those days the journey from northern New Hampshire to southernmost Georgia involved a long, hard trip by carriage or horseback, and voters were fortunate if they could find out something about their own local candidates, much less presidential nominees from distant regions. Then, too, there was the fear that some of the poorer people would become the willing tools of hotheads like Daniel Shays.

Elbridge Gerry proposed that the state governors pick the president; other delegates wanted the state legislatures to have this role. Both proposals were voted down. Instead, the Founding Fathers finally adopted the suggestion by James Wilson that the chief executive be elected by a roundabout system involving an "electoral college." This system provided that each state should choose electors equal in number to the state's senators and representatives in Congress. Then the electors would each cast two votes. The candidate who gained the largest number of votes would be president, and the candidate with the second largest number would be vice-president (The election of the vice-president was changed by the Twelfth Amendment; see pages 116-118.)

Each state legislature was free to set up its own method of electing the presidential electors. It could select them itself, or it could allow the people to elect them. (Today every state permits the people to choose its electors, who then cast the official votes in presidential and vice-presidential races.)

The Constitution makers set up the following qualifications for the president: this person must be at least thirty-five years of age, a natural-born citizen or a citizen at the time of the adoption of the Constitution, and a resident within the United States for at least fourteen years.

The president was given the power to administer and enforce laws made by Congress, conduct foreign affairs and draw up treaties, command the army, navy, and state militias when called into national service, appoint executive and judicial officers, reprieve or pardon persons accused of crimes, and veto bills passed by Congress. The powers given to the president were considered too extensive by many Americans in 1787. They provided one of the chief arguments for those that led the fight against ratification of the Constitution.

The Founding Fathers paid little attention to the office of the vice-president, who was given only one official duty: to preside over the Senate. Nor did they make it clear whether the vice-president would become president in the event of the president's death, resignation, or removal from office by impeachment. The right of the vice-president to assume the office of president was first asserted by John Tyler in 1841 after the death of President William Henry Harrison, and it became an established custom until 1967, when the Twenty-fifth Amendment formally approved this practice.

THE JUDICIAL BRANCH

The delegates to the Constitutional Convention knew that they wanted a "national judiciary," as suggested in the Virginia Plan. So they included in the Constitution provisions for a Supreme Court and other, inferior courts. But they let Congress decide most of the details involving the judicial branch of the government.

The first Congress passed the Judiciary Act of 1789, which set up the federal (national) court system that has functioned ever since. The lowest courts, called district courts, try most cases involving national laws. Above the district courts are the circuit courts, whose chief business is to hear cases that have been appealed from district courts on the basis that there was an error or injustice in the original decision. If either side in a lawsuit wants to appeal a decision of the circuit court, the case is then submitted to the Supreme Court, which may or may not agree to consider the case.

Congress also decides the number of justices (judges) on the Supreme Court. The original Supreme Court had a chief justice and five associate justices. In 1801 its membership was reduced to five; then it was set at seven in 1807, at nine in 1837, at ten in 1863, and at eight in 1866. In 1869 the number was fixed at nine justices, where it has remained ever since.

At the Constitutional Convention John Dickinson proposed that judges "may be removed by the Executive on the application by the Senate and the House of Representatives." Other delegates objected strenuously, contending that this proposal would make the third branch of the government subservient to the other two branches. James Wilson foresaw that "the judges would be in a bad situation, if made to depend on every gust of faction which might prevail in two branches of government." So it was decided that federal judges "shall hold their offices during good behavior," which meant they could stay on the bench for life or until they retired (unless convicted on an impeachment charge).

The chief function of the federal judiciary under the Constitution is clear: to hear cases arising under the Constitution, federal laws, and treaties. But the power of the federal judiciary that is most significant today is not specifically spelled out in the Constitution: to decide whether a national or state law is in accord with the Constitution. The Founding Fathers implied that the judges were to have this power in Article VI of the Constitution, which asserts that the Constitution, the laws, and the treaties of the United States "shall be the supreme Law of the Land and the Judges in every State shall be bound thereby." Nevertheless, the power of judges to declare laws unconstitutional did not become an established tradition until Chief Justice John Marshall first exercised this power in 1803 (see page 109).

The United States Senate in session in 1985.

CHECKS AND BALANCES

While the Constitution established three separate and distinct branches of the national government, it did not make these branches completely independent of one another. Instead, each branch is subject to a series of constitutional *checks* (restraints), which one or both of the other two branches may exercise against it. Furthermore, the powers to govern are *balanced* fairly equally among the three branches. The Founding Fathers provided this system of checks and balances to prevent any one branch of the government from becoming all-powerful.

The Constitution interlaces the three branches with several checks on their powers. Congress, for example, has the power to make laws, but the president may veto an act of Congress. And, in turn, Congress may pass legislation over a president's veto by a two-thirds vote of both houses. Moreover, Congress may make laws, but the Supreme Court has assumed the power to decide whether laws, if contested, are unconstitutional.

Congress may refuse to appropriate funds requested by the president, and the Senate may refuse to ratify treaties the president has made. The president may appoint all federal judges and officers in the executive department, but they must be approved by the Senate. Federal judges have a life tenure, but they and the executive officeholders, including the president, are subject to impeachment by Congress. Even the Senate and the House have checks on each other: both houses must pass a bill in identical language before it can be sent to the president for his signature and then become a law.

The system of checks and balances has now been in effect for about two centuries, and through the years it has worked remarkably well.

9

The Bill of Rights

James Madison kept his promise. He was elected to the first House of Representatives, and shortly after the House started to function in April 1789, Madison began work on the Bill of Rights—which he and other Federalists had promised to several states in return for their ratifying the Constitution.

These rights would be added at the end of the Constitution in the form of amendments. The Founding Fathers had included in the Constitution a procedure for amending it. An amendment could be proposed in one of two ways: by a two-thirds vote of both houses of Congress or through a convention called by Congress at the request of two-thirds of the state legislatures. Then the amendment must be ratified by three-fourths of the states. This could be done either by state legislatures or by state conventions called for that purpose. (Only one amendment, the Twenty-first, has been ratified by state conventions.)

Madison had to show both patience and perseverance in shepherding the Bill of Rights through Congress. He set May 25 as the date for introducing the subject in the House, but the representatives were in the midst of considering revenue measures, so they brushed aside Madison's request. Two weeks later he urged that the House take up the matter without further delay, but his colleagues continued to ignore his plea. On July 21 he introduced the topic again, and this time the House referred it to a committee that included Madison.

The first proposal by Madison included nine rights, based chiefly on the Declaration of Rights in the Virginia constitution. The committee expanded the nine articles to seventeen and referred them back to the House, which stalled for more than a month. Finally, on August 24, the House gave its approval and sent the seventeen amendments to the Senate.

The Senate whittled the number of amendments down to twelve, mainly by combining several points. After these amendments were passed by the Senate, they had to go to a conference committee made up of members from both houses. Differences between House and Senate versions were resolved, and the twelve amendments were approved by both houses. Then on September 25, 1789, they were sent on to the states for ratification.

Two of the twelve amendments were not ratified by the states. One of them proposed a (now outdated) formula to spell out how congressional seats would be allocated. The other amendment stated: *"No law varying the compensation for the services of the Senators and Representatives shall take effect, until an election of Representatives shall have intervened."*

Ironically, this amendment to forbid members of Congress to raise their own pay until after an election intervened is still alive today and gaining popular support. By a quirk of history, it carries no deadline for ratification, as proposed amendments do today. When the amendment was originally submitted to the states, only six ratified it. The amendment was then forgotten until 1816, when Congress raised its pay—from six dollars a day when in session to fifteen hundred dollars a year—and the states threatened to revive it. But so many incumbents, including Daniel Webster, were turned out of office by outraged voters that the new Congress canceled its pay hike.

James Madison contributed many of the ideas incorporated into the Constitution, kept the most thorough journal of the Constitutional Convention, and led the fight for the Bill of Rights in the House of Representatives.

Ohio ratified this amendment in 1873, and then it lay dormant for 105 years until 1978, when Wyoming followed suit. In recent years more states, concerned about rising congressional pay, have jumped on the bandwagon. By the summer of 1985 thirteen of the necessary thirty-eight states had ratified the amendment, and nine other states had ratification proposals pending.

The other ten original amendments were ratified by the necessary eleven of fourteen states (Vermont had joined the Union in March 1791) in a little over two years. New Jersey approved them first, on November 20, 1789. The eleventh state, Virginia, on December 15, 1791, ratified the ten amendments, thus making the Bill of Rights a part of the Constitution.

Curiously, three of the original thirteen states did not ratify the Bill of Rights until the 150th anniversary of its submission to the states. Massachusetts ratified on March 2, 1939, Georgia on March 18, 1939, and Connecticut on April 19, 1939.

The Bill of Rights emphasizes the basic principle of the Declaration of Independence: that the chief purpose of government is to protect individual rights. These constitutional amendments were designed to make sure that the new federal government would not abuse its great powers by oppressing the people it served. Keep in mind that the Bill of Rights protects individual rights only against possible abuses by the *national* government. The Fourteenth Amendment, which was adopted in 1868, has been interpreted by the Supreme Court to protect personal rights against possible abuses by *state* governments (see pages 111-114).

AMENDMENT 1

Congress shall make no law respecting an establishment of religion, or prohibiting the free exercise thereof; or abridging the freedom of speech, or of the press; or the right of the people peaceably to assemble, and to petition the government for a redress of grievances.

This very important amendment has some vital safeguards for the American people. It prohibits Congress from establishing any religion for the nation. People are free to worship as they please. They are free to say, write, or print almost anything they wish to communicate. They may meet peaceably with others, and through petitions they can ask the government to correct something they think is wrong.

These individual rights, however, are subject to certain limitations in cases where they might hurt other people. For example, your right to freedom of speech does not permit you falsely to shout "Fire!" in a crowded theater where the resulting panic could cause others to be injured or even killed. Nor does it allow you to make untruthful statements that will damage another person's reputation. During the past two centuries the courts have had to rule on many cases in which the civil rights of persons and the needs of society have been in conflict (see Chapter 10).

AMENDMENT 2

A well-regulated militia being necessary to the security of a free state, the right of the people to keep and bear arms shall not be infringed.

This amendment primarily sprang from the concern in 1789 that the leaders of a large national army might try to crush the people's rights. Fearing such an army, the people demanded the right to have state militias. (Today the National Guard, or militia, of each state is made up of volunteers who live in that state.) The Second Amendment does not prohibit laws against owning or carrying unlicensed guns and "concealed weapons."

AMENDMENT 3

No soldier shall, in time of peace, be quartered in any house, without the consent of the owner; nor in time of war, but in a manner to be prescribed by law.

In colonial days the British government often forced Americans to take soldiers into their homes and give them food and a place to sleep. The colonists bitterly resented this practice, and the Third Amendment assured citizens that the American government would not quarter soldiers in their houses.

AMENDMENT 4

The right of the people to be secure in their persons, house, papers, and effects, against unreasonable searches and seizures, shall not be violated; and no warrants shall issue, but upon probable cause, supported by oath or affirmation, and particularly describing the place to be searched, and the persons or things to be seized.

An old English law said that government officers could not arrest a person or search his house without the legal right to do so. This reflected the long-established principle that "a man's house is his castle." But before the Revolutionary War, British officials had used "writs of assistance" (general search warrants that did not specify the items that were sought) to hunt for smuggled goods. They also illegally arrested suspicious persons.

This amendment was designed to forbid American officials to commit the same abuses.

AMENDMENT 5

No person shall be held to answer for a capital, or otherwise infamous crime, unless on a presentment or indictment of a Grand Jury, except in cases arising in the land or naval forces, or in the militia, when in actual service in time of war or public danger; nor shall any person be subject for the same offense to be twice put in jeopardy of life or limb; nor shall be compelled in any criminal cases to be a witness against himself, nor be deprived of life, liberty, or property, without due process of law; not shall private property be taken for public use, without just compensation.

Amendments 5 through 8 have been called the "Bill of Rights for accused persons." The first part of the Fifth Amendment means that the federal government cannot try a person for a serious crime until a grand jury decides that there is enough evidence against that person to warrant his or her being brought to trial.

The statement that a person cannot be "twice put in jeopardy" means that someone who has been tried for a crime in a federal court and found not guilty cannot be tried again by the federal government for the same crime. The provision that no one shall be compelled in a criminal case to be "a witness against himself" means that an accused person cannot be forced to take the stand in a trial or answer any questions that might be used against him or her in criminal prosecutions. This right to refuse to testify on grounds of self-incrimination extends to witnesses at trials and hearings before congressional committees.

The "due process" clause means that the government cannot execute or imprison a person or take away that person's property except according to fair methods under the law. The final provision in this amendment prevents the government from taking private property for public use (such as for a freeway or a park) unless it pays the owner a fair price for the property.

AMENDMENT 6

In all criminal prosecutions, the accused shall enjoy the right to a speedy and public trial, by an impartial jury of the State and district wherein the crime shall have been committed, which district shall have been previously ascertained by law, and to be informed of the nature and cause of the accusation; to be confronted with the witnesses against him; to have compulsory process for obtaining witnesses in his favor, and to have the assistance of counsel for his defense.

In earlier days persons suspected of crimes sometimes were thrown into jail without knowing the charges against them and were allowed to stay there for long periods of time before their cases came to trial. The Sixth Amendment provides that a person must be told why he or she has been arrested and must be given a speedy and public trial. The accused person (defendant) has the right to be tried by an impartial jury and to confront all the witnesses and hear their testimony, including "cross-examination" by the defendant's attorney. The defendant may call to the stand his or her own witnesses and be provided a lawyer at government expense if he or she cannot afford to pay for a lawyer.

AMENDMENT 7

In suits at common law, where the value in controversy shall exceed twenty dollars, the right of trial by jury shall be preserved, and no fact tried by a jury, shall be otherwise re-examined in any court of the United States, than according to the rules of the common law.

Amendment 7 refers to civil cases, not criminal cases. Civil cases usually deal with disagreements about persons' rights and duties toward one another. In some civil suits a jury may be dispensed with if both parties agree to let the judge make the decision and the judge agrees to do so.

When a civil case has been appealed from a lower to higher court, the judge or judges of the higher court may change the verdict in the lower court only if the exact meaning of the law was not interpreted correctly in the lower court or if the jury (or judge) reached its verdict without having sufficient evidence. The higher court may reduce the amount of money awarded by a jury to the plaintiff who brought the suit.

AMENDMENT 8

Excessive bail shall not be required, nor excessive fines imposed, nor cruel and unusual punishments inflicted.

"Bail" is the money that the accused person must hand over to the court in order to go free until the trial begins. The bail is returned when the trial has ended. Amendment 8 orders that federal judges must not demand unfair amounts of bail.

In colonial times cruel forms of punishment were common. Guilty persons, for example, often were put in stocks in which wooden blocks were clamped around their arms, their legs, and sometimes their necks. Or the court might sentence them to have their thumbs branded by a hot iron or their backs lashed by a heavy leather strap. When this amendment was being debated in the House of Representatives, one congressman objected to it because he said it was sometimes necessary to cut off the ears of criminals.

Amendment 8 prohibits people convicted of a crime from being punished by any kind of torture or fined more than is fair. Even today, Americans are still debating whether the death penalty is a "cruel" and "unusual" punishment for someone who commits a serious crime, such as murder. But the Supreme Court has ruled that it is not cruel or unusual if state legislatures fix strict and fair guidelines for judges and juries to follow when imposing the death penalty.

AMENDMENT 9

The enumeration in the Constitution, of certain rights, shall not be construed to deny or disparage others retained by the people.

The first eight amendments list certain, but not all, rights of the people. Amendment 9 was added so that the federal government would not interfere with any other rights that are not specified in the Bill of Rights. Through Court interpretations these now include such things as the people's right to privacy and the right to take part in political activities.

AMENDMENT 10

The powers not delegated to the United States by the Constitution, nor prohibited by it to the States, are reserved to the States respectively, or to the people.

The other nine amendments in the Bill of Rights deal with the rights of the individual. The Tenth Amendment protects the states as well as the people. It asserts that all powers not given to the national government by the Constitution belong to the states or the people. This amendment defines the meaning of our federal system of government.

10

Interpreting the Constitution

In the early days of our republic the Supreme Court assumed the power to declare acts of Congress and the state legislatures unconstitutional.

The first Congress enacted the Judiciary Act of 1789, and in 1801 William Marbury sued James Madison on the basis of a provision in this act. Marbury had been appointed a justice of the peace but had not received his commission to serve on the bench, so he filed a lawsuit against Madison, the secretary of state, for not delivering his commission. By a unanimous vote the Supreme Court refused Marbury's request. Chief Justice John Marshall, speaking for the Court, said that the justices had found the pertinent section of the Judiciary Act in conflict with the Constitution and, therefore, void. Then Marshall firmly asserted, "It is emphatically the province and duty of the judicial department to say what the law is."

Thus, *Marbury* v. *Madison* (1803) established the important principle known as judicial review. This means that the courts may determine the constitutionality of laws, and those that are unconstitutional cannot be enforced. Most of our nation's courts, federal and state, may exercise the extremely important power of judicial review. But the ultimate exercise of this power rests with the Supreme Court; it is the final authority on the meaning of the Constitution.

Between 3,500 and 4,000 cases are appealed to the Supreme Court every year. In a large number of these cases, the petitions for review are denied, generally because all or at least the majority of the justices agree with the decision of the lower court or feel no important point of law is involved. More than half of the cases decided by the Supreme Court are disposed of in brief orders and without hearing arguments. Often a case is returned to a lower court for further consideration in the light of some other related case decided earlier by the Court. All in all, the Supreme Court decides, after hearing arguments and writing full opinions, about 120 cases each year.

The Court rules on the constitutionality of very few of all the laws passed by Congress and the state legislatures. Generally speaking, someone has to break a law and claim that it violates the Constitution before the Court applies judicial review.

Although the Supreme Court can be likened to a head umpire, sometimes it reverses itself. Times change, and so do the justices on the bench. For example, in 1896 the Supreme Court in *Plessy* v. *Ferguson* upheld a Louisiana law requiring the segregation of blacks and whites in separate railroad cars. The Court ruled that the Louisiana law did not violate the "equal protection" clause of the Fourteenth Amendment as long as the *separate* facilities for blacks were *equal* to those provided for whites. This "separate but equal" doctrine was soon extended to other areas as constitutional justification for racial segregation, and it stood largely unchallenged for nearly sixty years.

Finally, in 1954, the Supreme Court did an about-face and reversed *Plessy* v. *Ferguson,* claiming that the forced separation of races did indeed violate the "equal protection" clause. In *Brown* v. *Topĕka Board of Education* the Court struck down the laws of four states requiring or allowing separate public schools for black and white students. Asserting that segregation of the races in public education is unconstitutional, Chief Justice Earl Warren said for a unanimous Supreme Court: "We conclude that in the field of public education the doctrine of 'separate but equal' has no place. Separate educational facilities are inherently unequal."

Wiretapping without a search warrant is another field in which the Supreme Court has reversed itself. In 1928 the Court dealt with wiretapping for the first time, in the case of *Olmstead* v. *United States.* Chief Justice William Howard Taft, writing for the majority of justices, claimed that wiretapping did not violate the Fourth Amendment because it did not involve search and seizure. There had been no illegal entry, he wrote, because that tap had been placed outside the accused person's property. Only the spoken word had been seized, and, in the judgment of the Court, the spoken word was not protected by the Fourth Amendment.

Nearly forty years later the Supreme Court looked at a similar situation in a different way. In *Katz* v. *United States,* in 1967, the Court declared that "the Fourth Amendment protects people, not places" and decreed that wiretapping without a search warrant is unconstitutional.

Many of the cases that have reached the Supreme Court in the past two centuries have involved the protection of personal rights. Long ago James Madison foresaw the need to guard the individual against the possible encroachment of a powerful government. "In framing a government which is to be administered by men over men," Madison said, "the great difficulty lies in this: you must first enable the government to control the governed; and in the next place oblige it to control itself." But before 1925 the Supreme Court maintained that its power to protect the individual was almost entirely restricted to cases in which the *national* government was charged with violating the Bill of Rights.

In 1925, however, the long process began whereby the Court "read into the meaning" of the Fourteenth Amendment most of the protections guaranteed in the Bill of Rights—and thus made them applicable against the *states.* The 1925 landmark case was *Gitlow* v. *New York,* in which the Court proclaimed that freedom of speech was "among the fundamental personal rights protected by the due process clause of the Fourteenth Amendment."

Soon there followed additional cases in which the Supreme Court expanded the scope of the Fourteenth Amendment. These included protections against state governments in regard to freedom of the press (1931), freedom of assembly and petition (1937), and freedom of religion (1940).

Later, in the 1960s, the Supreme Court ruled that each of these guarantees in the Bill of Rights applied to the state governments, too: the Fourth Amendment's prohibition of unreasonable searches and seizures and the refusal to accept in courts any evidence gained by those actions (1961); the Sixth Amendment's guarantee that the accused person may have a lawyer, whose fees must be paid by the government if the defendant cannot afford to pay them (1963); the Fifth Amendment's ban on self-incrimination (1964); the Sixth Amendment's right of a person accused of a crime to confront the witnesses called to the stand by the prosecuting lawyer (1965); the Sixth Amendment's right of the suspect to remain silent and to be told that anything he or she said could be used as evidence in court (1966); the Sixth Amendment's promise of a speedy trial (1967); the Sixth Amendment's guarantee that the defendant may compel witnesses to take the stand in his or her behalf (1967); the Sixth Amendment's guarantee of trial by jury (1968); and the Fifth Amendment's prohibition of double jeopardy (1969).

During the 1970s and 1980s the Supreme Court continued to rule on many cases involving human rights. In the summer of 1985, for example, the Court handed down four separate decisions that were all based on the First Amendment's separation of church and state (as applied to the states by the Fourteenth Amendment). In all four instances the Court reasserted this test it had adopted in 1971 to mark the line dividing church and state: to be acceptable, a law must have a secular (nonreligious) purpose; it must neither advance nor inhibit (obstruct) religion; and it must not excessively entangle government with religion. Using this yardstick as its guide, the Supreme Court struck down an Alabama law that set aside a moment of silence in public school classrooms for voluntary prayer, a Connecticut law that required employers to give their workers the right to refuse to work on the Sabbath, a New York City program that used federal funds for teaching secular subjects to poor students in church schools, and a program that used state and local funds to teach remedial and enrichment courses in religious schools in Grand Rapids, Michigan.

The Supreme Court justices pictured here are Sandra Day O'Connor, Lewis Powell, Thurgood Marshall, William Brennan, Jr., Chief Justice William Rehnquist, Byron White, Harry Blackmun, John Paul Stevens, and Antonin Scalia.

Some Americans disapproved of these and other Court decisions. President Ronald Reagan was the spokesman for millions of citizens when he sternly rebuked Court rulings that struck down school prayers and upheld abortions. In a July 1985 address before the American Bar Association, Attorney General Edwin Meese III criticized the Supreme Court's neutrality toward religion and suggested that it would have struck the Founding Fathers as "somewhat bizarre." Meese declared that the purpose of the First Amendment's ban on the establishment of religion "was to prohibit religious tyranny, not to undermine religion generally."

Both critics and supporters of Supreme Court decisions recognize that former Chief Justice Charles Evans Hughes was correct when he said, "The Constitution means what the judges say it means." But critics often feel frustrated because it is so difficult to overrule Court verdicts. President Franklin D. Roosevelt was frustrated by the Supreme Court when it declared some of his major New Deal projects unconstitutional. So he tried to get Congress to increase the size of the Supreme Court, thereby permitting him to name additional justices who would reflect his views. But Congress balked at FDR's attempt to "pack" the Supreme Court with his supporters.

Nevertheless, Supreme Court decisions provide one of the two ways to adapt the Constitution to modern times. The Court, according to Woodrow Wilson, can be viewed as a "constitutional convention in continuous session." The other way to keep the Constitution up-to-date is to use the amending process.

11

Changing the Constitution, 1798-1870

Why are amendments to the Constitution made? They generally are drawn up to add new provisions to the Constitution (such as the Bill of Rights), to change existing provisions in the Constitution, or to nullify decisions made by the Supreme Court.

Over six thousand resolutions proposing amendments have been submitted to the Congress since 1789. Congress, however, has approved and sent on to the states only thirty-three of them. And of these, only twenty-six have been ratified. The first ten of these amendments (the Bill of Rights) became effective in 1791. Since then only sixteen additional amendments have been added to the Constitution.

AMENDMENT 11 (adopted in 1798)

The judicial power of the United States shall not be construed to extend to any suit in law or equity, commenced or prosecuted against one of the United States by citizens of another State, or by citizens or subjects of any foreign state.

This was the first amendment to strike down a provision in the Constitution, and it also nullified a Supreme Court decision. Article III, Section 2 of the Constitution let federal courts try cases between a state and citizens of foreign countries. In the early days of our republic, many Americans felt that these provisions gave too much power to the federal courts.

The matter came to a head in 1793 when the Supreme Court upheld claims against the state of Georgia by the heirs of a British man whose property had been confiscated (seized) in the Revolutionary War. This made the Georgia House of Representatives so irate that it passed a bill saying that any official who tried to enforce the Supreme Court's decision should be declared guilty of a felony and immediately hanged.

So, owing to public pressure, the Eleventh Amendment was added to the Constitution, prohibiting a citizen of one state or of a foreign country from suing another state in a federal court. Such suits are tried in state courts.

AMENDMENT 12 (adopted in 1804)

The Electors shall meet in their respective states, and vote by ballot for President, and Vice-President, one of whom, at least, shall not be an inhabitant of the same state with themselves; they shall name in their ballots the person voted for as President and in distinct ballots the person voted for as Vice-President, and they shall make distinct lists of all persons voted for as President, and of all persons voted for as Vice-President, and of the number of votes for each, which lists they shall sign and certify, and transmit sealed to the seat of the government of the United States, directed to the President of the Senate;—The President of the Senate shall, in the presence of the Senate and House of Representatives, open all the certificates and the votes shall then be counted;—The person having the greatest number of votes for President, shall be the President, if such number be a majority of the whole number of Electors appointed; and if no person have such majority, then from the persons having the highest numbers not exceeding three on the list of those voted for as President, the House of Representatives shall choose immediately, by ballot, the President. But in choosing the President, the votes shall be taken by States, the representation from each State having one vote; a quorum for this purpose shall consist of a member or members from two-thirds of the States, and a majority of all the States shall be necessary to a choice. And if the House of Representatives shall not choose a President whenever the right of choice shall devolve upon them, before the fourth day of March[1] next following, then the Vice-President shall act as President, as in the case of the death or other constitutional disability of the President.—The person having the greatest number of votes as Vice-President, shall be the Vice-President, if such number be a majority of the whole number of Electors appointed, and if no person have a majority, then from the two highest numbers on the list, the Senate shall choose the Vice-President; a quorum for the purpose shall consist of two-thirds of the whole number of Senators, and a majority of the whole number shall be necessary to a choice. But no person constitutionally ineligible to the office of President shall be eligible to that of Vice-President of the United States.

When the Constitution was written there were no political parties. There was just one election for both president and vice-president, and each elector had two votes. The Founding Fathers assumed that the candidate with the most votes would be elected president and the runner-up would be vice-president.

With the emergence of political parties, all the electors of the Democratic-Republican party wanted to give one of their two electoral votes to the presidential candidate of their party and the other to their party's vice-presidential candidate. When this occurred in 1800, the presidential and vice-presidential candidates of the Democratic-Republican party, Thomas Jefferson and Aaron Burr, tied in the electoral vote. So the election had to be decided by the House of Representatives, which elected Jefferson president and Burr vice-president.

The Twelfth Amendment ended this electoral confusion by specifying that the president and vice-president must be elected on separate ballots. Since 1800 only one other presidential election (in 1824) has been decided by the House of Representatives, and that was because no candidate had a majority of the electoral vote. At that time, in accord with another provision of the Twelfth Amendment, the three candidates with the most electoral votes—Andrew Jackson, John Quincy Adams, and William Crawford—were voted upon by

---

[1]Changed to January 20 by the Twentieth Amendment.

the House, with each state having one vote. Adams was elected president.

As a last-ditch effort to avert the Civil War a remarkable amendment was proposed by Congress in 1861. It was then signed by President James Buchanan on March 2, 1861, two days before his term ended and Abraham Lincoln moved into the White House. (An amendment does not require the president's signature, and this was the only proposed amendment ever signed by a president.) It said: "No amendment shall be made to the Constitution which will authorize or give to Congress the power to abolish or interfere, within any State, with the domestic institutions thereof, including that of persons held to labor or service by the laws of said State."

This proposed amendment, which never was ratified, would have protected slavery in the Constitution. It would have been the Thirteenth Amendment. Ironically, the Thirteenth Amendment, adopted after the Civil War, did just the opposite—it freed all the slaves.

AMENDMENT 13 (adopted in 1865)

Section 1. *Neither slavery nor involuntary servitude, except as a punishment for crime whereof the party shall have been duly convicted, shall exist within the United States, or any place subject to their jurisdiction.*

Section 2. *Congress shall have power to enforce this article by appropriate legislation.*

When this amendment was first proposed in April 1864—at a time when the southern states that belonged to the Confederacy had no representation in Congress—it was approved in the Senate, but it failed to receive the required two-thirds vote in the House. It was proposed again in January 1865, about three months before the end of the Civil War, and passed in both houses, but a switch of only three votes in the House would have again blocked approval.

AMENDMENT 14 (adopted in 1868)

Section 1. *All persons born or naturalized in the United States, and subject to the jurisdiction thereof, are citizens of the*

United States and of the State wherein they reside. No state shall make or enforce any law which shall abridge the privileges or immunities of citizens of the United States; nor shall any State deprive any person of life, liberty, or property, without due process of law; nor deny to any person within its jurisdiction the equal protection of the laws.

The original purpose of the first section of the Fourteenth Amendment was to make citizens of the former slaves and to prohibit the states from taking away their rights of citizenship. But in the twentieth century, particularly since the 1960s, the Supreme Court's interpretation of this section of the Fourteenth Amendment has been greatly expanded and has acquired enormous significance.

While the Bill of Rights forbids only the national government from interfering with people's rights, the Supreme Court has applied this part of the Fourteenth Amendment to also prevent state governments from interfering with people's rights: *"nor shall any State deprive any person of life, liberty, or property without due process of law, nor deny any person within its jurisdiction the equal protection of the laws."* In a long series of cases the Supreme Court has ruled that most of the specific guarantees in the Bill of Rights are also protected in the Fourteenth Amendment's "due process" and "equal protection" clauses. (Some of these cases are discussed on pages 111-114.)

Section 2. *Representatives shall be apportioned among the several States according to the respective numbers, counting the whole number of persons in each State, excluding Indians not taxed. But when the right to vote at any election for the choice of Electors for President and Vice-President of the United States, Representatives in Congress, the executive and judicial officers of a State, or the members of the legislature thereof, is denied to any of the male inhabitants of such State, being twenty-one years of age and citizens of the United States, or in any way abridged, except for participation in rebellion, or other crime, the basis of representation therein shall be reduced in the proportion which the number of such male citizens shall bear to the whole number of male citizens twenty-one years of age in such State.*

Before the Fourteenth Amendment was adopted, only three-fifths of the black slaves had been counted in determining how many seats each state would have in the House of Representatives. This amendment ruled that everyone was to be counted except for Indians, who were not taxed. It further provided that if any state denied the right of its citizens to vote for federal or state offices, the number of its representatives in the House should be decreased in proportion to the number of adult male citizens denied the vote.

Section 3. *No person shall be a Senator or Representative in Congress, or Elector of President and Vice-President, or hold any office, civil or military, under the United States, or under any State, who, having previously taken an oath, as a member of Congress, or as an officer of the United States, or as a member of any State legislature, or as an executive or judicial officer of any State, to support the Constitution of the United States, shall have engaged in insurrection or rebellion against the same, or given aid or comfort to the enemies thereof. But Congress may, be a vote of two-thirds of each house, remove such disability.*

The third section of Amendment 14 prohibited anyone who had helped the Confederacy in the Civil War from holding federal or state office (unless authorized by Congress) if before the war that person had taken an oath to support the United States Constitution. This meant that most of the South's leaders before the Civil War were denied the opportunity to hold government offices unless or until they were given this right by Congress. In 1872 Congress pardoned many of the men who had served the Confederacy, and in 1898 it ended this punishment for the other former Confederates.

Section 4. *The validity of the public debt of the United States, authorized by law, including debts incurred for payment of pensions and bounties for services in suppressing insurrection or rebellion, shall not be questioned. But neither the United States nor any State shall assume or pay any debt or obligation incurred in aid of insurrection or rebellion against the United States, or any claim for the loss or emancipation of any slave; but all such debts, obligations, and claims shall be held illegal and void.*

Section 5. *The Congress shall have power to enforce, by appropriate legislation, the provisions of this article.*

The first part of Section 4 authorized the national government to pay back the debts it had acquired as a result of the Civil War. The second part of Section 4 prohibited the federal government and the states from paying back any money the Confederacy had borrowed to wage the war.

When the amendment was sent to the states for ratification, it was turned down by nine of the former Confederate states. Only after Congress enacted a law making such ratification a condition for being readmitted to the Union did these states approve the amendment.

AMENDMENT 15 (adopted in 1870)

Section 1. *The right of citizens of the United States to vote shall not be denied or abridged by the United States or by any State on account of race, color, or previous condition of servitude.*

Section 2. *The Congress shall have power to enforce this article by appropriate legislation.*

Even though the Fourteenth Amendment called for reducing representation in the House of states that failed to let black males vote, this threat was generally ignored in the South. So the Fifteenth Amendment was added to the Constitution to prevent states from denying the vote to a male citizen "on account of race, color, or previous condition of servitude [slavery]." Many southern states, however, continued to find ways to keep blacks from voting. Finally, beginning in 1957, Congress passed successively stronger laws designed to end racial discrimination in voting.

The picture of a black man voting for the first time in *Harper's Weekly* on November 16, 1867.

12

Changing the Constitution in the Twentieth Century

After the Fifteenth Amendment was ratified in 1870, forty-three years passed before the next amendment was added to the Constitution. Then, during the next seven-year period (1913–1920), four additional amendments were ratified. They are sometimes called the "progressive amendments" because they reflect the spirit of reform that was sweeping across the nation in the early part of the twentieth century.

AMENDMENT 16 (adopted in 1913)

The Congress shall have power to lay and collect taxes on incomes, from whatever source derived, without apportionment among the several States, and without regard to any census or enumeration.

In 1894 Congress passed a law calling for an income tax. But in 1895 the Supreme Court declared the income tax unconstitutional because it violated a provision in the Constitution which states that the federal government may levy no direct tax except in proportion to each state's population. A direct tax, such as a property tax, is one that must be paid directly by the person upon whom it is imposed. Since the only legal way to overrule a Supreme Court decision is to add an amendment to the Constitution, Congress proposed the income tax amendment in 1909, and it was ratified four years later. Today the federal government gets more of its revenue by taxing incomes than it gets in any other way.

AMENDMENT 17 (adopted in 1913)

Section 1. *The Senate of the United States shall be composed of two Senators from each State, elected by the people thereof, for six years; and each Senator shall have one vote. The electors in each State shall have the qualifications requisite for electors of* [voters for] *the most numerous branch of the State legislatures.*

Section 2. *When vacancies happen in the representation of any State in the Senate, the executive authority of such State shall issue writs of election to fill such vacancies: Provided, that the Legislature of any State may empower the executive thereof to make temporary appointments until the people fill the vacancies by election as the Legislature may direct.*

Section 3. *This amendment shall not be so construed as to affect the election or term of any Senator chosen before it becomes valid as part of the Constitution.*

This amendment, permitting the people to vote directly for their United States senators, replaces the section of the Constitution that authorized state legislatures to choose senators. It also provides that states may empower their governors to appoint persons to fill unexpired terms of senators when vacancies occur.

AMENDMENT 18 (adopted in 1919)

Section 1. *After one year from the ratification of this article the manufacture, sale, or transportation of intoxicating liquors within, the importation thereof into, or the exportation thereof from the United States and all territory subject to the jurisdiction thereof, for beverage purposes, is hereby prohibited.*

Section 2. *The Congress and the several States shall have concurrent power to enforce this article by appropriate legislation.*

Section 3. *This article shall be inoperative unless it shall have been ratified as an amendment to the Constitution by the legislatures of the several States, as provided by the Constitution, within seven years from the date of the submission thereof to the States by the Congress.*

The Eighteenth Amendment, commonly called the Prohibition Amendment, forbade the manufacture, sale, and transportation of intoxicating liquors for persons to drink. (It was repealed by the Twenty-first Amendment in 1933.)

AMENDMENT 19 (adopted in 1920)

Section 1. *The right of citizens of the United States to vote shall not be denied or abridged by the United States or by any State on account of sex.*

Section 2. *The Congress shall have power to enforce this article by appropriate legislation.*

The struggle for women to gain the vote was long and difficult. At the Woman's Rights Convention that met in 1848 at Seneca Falls, New York, a resolution was passed demanding the ballot for women. But at that time neither the federal government nor the states took any action on woman suffrage (the right to vote). Finally, in 1869, Wyoming, while still a territory, gave women the vote. Later, in 1890, Wyoming also became the first state to permit woman suffrage. By 1917 equal suffrage was granted in twelve states.

Meanwhile, there was a movement in Congress to pass a constitutional amendment that would give the vote to women throughout the nation. This amendment was first introduced in the Senate in 1878 and was reintroduced again and again for the next forty years.

In 1918, during World War I, the Nineteenth Amendment squeaked through the House of Representatives by a vote of 274 to 136, a bare two-thirds majority. President Woodrow Wilson, who maintained that the United States had entered the war to "save the world for democracy," made a special trip to the Senate on September 30, 1918, to urge passage of the amendment. He said this was "vitally essential to the successful prosecution of the great war of humanity in which we are engaged." The next day the stubborn Senate again voted down the amendment.

It was not until the spring of 1919, several months after the war had ended, that the Nineteenth Amendment cleared Congress, and in August 1920 it was ratified by enough states to go into operation.

AMENDMENT 20 (adopted in 1933)

Section 1. *The terms of the President and Vice-President shall end at noon on the 20th day of January, and the terms of Senators and Representatives at noon on the 3d day of January, of the years in which such terms would have ended if this article had not been ratified; and the terms of their successors shall then begin.*

Section 2. *The Congress shall assemble at least once in every year, and such meeting shall begin at noon on the 3d day of January, unless they shall by law appoint a different day.*

Before the Twentieth Amendment was added to the Constitution, a president defeated in the November election continued in office until the following March 4. Defeated senators and representatives also stayed in office until March 4, and members of the new Congress did not begin their terms until the next December, thirteen months after they had been elected.

The Twentieth Amendment ended the practice whereby federal officeholders who had been defeated at the polls kept their jobs for several months after the elections. (They were called "lame ducks.") According to this amendment, the president is inaugurated on January 20, and the new Congress meets on January 3.

Section 3. *If, at the time fixed for the beginning of the term of the President, the President-elect shall have died, the Vice-President-elect shall become President. If a President shall not have been chosen before the time fixed for the beginning of his term, or if the President-elect shall have failed to qualify, then the Vice-President-elect shall act as President until a*

Women's suffrage parades, such as this one in Washington, helped gain support for the Nineteenth Amendment.

President should have qualified; and the Congress may by law provide for the case wherein neither a President-elect nor a Vice-President-elect shall have qualified, declaring who shall then act as President, or the manner in which one who is to act shall be selected, and such persons shall act accordingly until a President or Vice-President shall have qualified.

Section 4. *The Congress may by law provide for the case of the death of any of the persons from whom the House of Representatives may choose a President whenever the right of choice shall have devolved upon them, and for the case of the death of any of the persons from whom the Senate may choose a Vice-President whenever the right of choice shall have devolved upon them.*

Section 5. *Sections 1 and 2 shall take effect on the 15th day of October following the ratification of this article.*

Section 6. *This article shall be inoperative unless it shall have been ratified as an amendment to the Constitution by the Legislatures of three-fourths of the several States within seven years from the date of its submission.*

The third section of the Twentieth Amendment gives the procedure to be followed if a newly elected president or vice-president should die or for some other reason should be unable to take office. The fourth section specifies what should be done if a candidate for the presidency dies while a close election is being settled in the House of Representatives, or a candidate for the vice-presidency dies while a close election is being decided in the Senate.

AMENDMENT 21 (adopted in 1933)

Section 1. *The eighteenth article of amendment to the Constitution of the United States is hereby repealed.*

Section 2. *The transportation or importation into any State, Territory, or Possession of the United States for delivery or use therein of intoxicating liquors, in violation of the laws thereof, is hereby prohibited.*

Section 3. *This article shall be inoperative unless it shall have been ratified as an amendment to the Constitution by conventions in the several States, as provided in the Constitution, within seven years from the date of the submission thereof to the States by the Congress.*

Prohibition had not proved effective. It was difficult to enforce and led to an increase of organized crime. So the Twenty-first Amendment was added to the Constitution to repeal the Eighteenth Amendment. This was the only time in our history that one amendment was replaced entirely by another. Also, it was the only time that an amendment was ratified by state conventions instead of state legislatures, which was done in part to achieve speedy action. The Twenty-first Amendment was submitted to the states in February 1933 and, after ratification by the necessary three-fourths of the states, went into effect on December 5 of the same year.

AMENDMENT 22 (adopted in 1951)

Section 1. *No person shall be elected to the office of president more than twice, and no person who has held the office of President, or acted as President, for more than two years of a term to which some other person was elected President shall be elected to the office of President more than once. But this article shall not apply to any person holding the office of President when this article was proposed by the Congress* [i.e., Harry Truman], *and shall not prevent any person who may be holding the office of President, or acting as President, during the term within which this article becomes operative from holding the office of President or acting as President during the remainder of such term.*

Section 2. *This article shall be inoperative unless it shall have been ratified as an amendment to the Constitution by the legislatures of three-fourths of the several States within seven years from the date of its submission to the States by the Congress.*

Democrat Franklin D. Roosevelt had been elected to third and fourth terms as president. When the Republicans captured control of both the Senate and the House of Representatives in 1947, they pushed through Congress the Twenty-second Amendment, which prevented any other person from being elected to more than two full terms in the White House.

There is one situation, however, in which a president may serve for up to ten years. If a vice-president becomes president with less than two years of the former president's term remaining, he or she may be elected for two more full terms. But if the vice-president becomes president with more than two years of the former president's term remaining, he or she may be elected for only one more term. For example, when Vice-President Lyndon B. Johnson became president after President John F. Kennedy was assassinated in November 1963, Johnson could have run for two more terms because he would have served less than two years of Kennedy's term. On the other hand, when Vice-President Gerald Ford became president after President Richard Nixon resigned from office in August 1974, Ford could have run for only one more term because he would have served more than two years of Nixon's (second) term.

Some political scientists have criticized the Twenty-second Amendment because it deprives the people of the right to decide at the polls whether they want a president elected to a third term.

AMENDMENT 23 (adopted in 1961)

Section 1. *The District constituting the seat of Government of the United States shall appoint in such manner as the Congress may direct: A number of electors of President and Vice-President equal to the whole number of Senators and Representatives in Congress to which the District would be entitled if it were a State, but in no event more than the least populous State; they shall be in addition to those appointed by the States, but they shall be considered for the purposes of the election of President and Vice-President, to be electors appointed by a State; and they shall meet in the District and perform such duties as provided by the twelfth article of amendment.*

Section 2. *The Congress shall have the power to enforce this article by appropriate legislation.*

For many years the people who lived in the large city of Washington, D.C., could not vote for president or vice-president. Since our national capital is in a federal district that is not in any state, it has no senators or voting members of the House of Representatives, so it had no electoral votes until the Twenty-third Amendment became effective in 1961. The District of Columbia now has three electoral votes; since the 1964 election these three electoral votes have always been cast for the Democratic presidential and vice-presidential candidates.

AMENDMENT 24 (adopted in 1964)

Section 1. *The right of citizens of the United States to vote in any primary or other election for President or Vice-President, for electors for President or Vice-President, or for Senator or Representative in Congress, shall not be denied or abridged by the United States or any State by reason of failure to pay any poll tax or other tax.*

Section 2. *The Congress shall have the power to enforce this article by appropriate legislation.*

To discourage blacks from going to the polls, some southern states required the payment of a poll tax in order to vote. The Twenty-fourth Amendment forbids the poll tax as a requirement for voting in all federal elections (for president, vice-president, and members of Congress). This amendment says nothing about state elections, but the Voting Rights Act of 1965 directed the United States attorney general to contest in the courts the poll tax requirement in state and local elections. In 1966 the Supreme Court ruled that Virginia's poll tax requirement was unconstitutional because it violated the equal protection clause of the Fourteenth Amendment, and soon afterward the other states that collected poll taxes ended this practice.

AMENDMENT 25 (adopted in 1967)

Section 1. *In case of the removal of the President from office or of his death or resignation, the Vice-President shall become President.*

Section 2. *Whenever there is a vacancy in the office of the Vice-President, the President shall nominate a Vice-President who shall take office upon confirmation by a majority vote of both Houses of Congress.*

Seven presidents had been vice-presidents who succeeded to the presidency following the deaths of former presidents, and when this happened the office of vice-president was vacant. The second section of Amendment 25 says that when there is a vacancy in the office of vice-president, the president may nominate a vice-president, whose appointment must be confirmed by a majority vote of both houses of Congress.

The first appointed vice-president was Gerald Ford, a former congressman from Michigan. He was nominated for this position by President Richard Nixon following the resignation of Vice-President Spiro Agnew in October 1973. (Later Ford became president following the resignation of Nixon in August 1974.)

Section 3. Whenever the President transmits to the President pro tempore of the Senate and the Speaker of the House of Representatives his written declaration that he is unable to discharge the powers and duties of his office, and until he transmits to them a written declaration to the contrary, such powers and duties shall be discharged by the Vice-President as Acting President.

Section 4. Whenever the Vice-President and a majority of either the principal officers of the executive departments or of such other body as Congress may by law provide, transmit to the President pro tempore of the Senate and the Speaker of the House of Representatives their written declaration that the President is unable to discharge the powers and duties of his office, the Vice-President shall immediately assume the powers and duties of the office as Acting President.

Thereafter, when the President transmits to the President pro tempore of the Senate and the Speaker of the House of Representatives his written declaration that no inability exists, he shall resume the powers and duties of his office unless the Vice-President and a majority of either the principal officers of the executive departments or of such other body as Congress may by law provide, transmit within four days to the President pro tempore of the Senate and the Speaker of the House of Representatives their written declaration that the President is unable to discharge the powers and duties of his office. Thereupon Congress shall decide the issue, assembling within forty-eight hours for that purpose if not in session.

If the Congress, within twenty-one days after receipt of the latter written declaration, or, if Congress is not in session, within twenty-one days after Congress is required to assemble, determines by two-thirds vote of both Houses that the President is unable to discharge the powers and duties of his office, the Vice-President shall continue to discharge the same as Acting President; otherwise, the President shall resume the powers and duties of his office.

Three presidents—James A. Garfield, Woodrow Wilson, and Dwight D. Eisenhower—were stricken with long, serious illnesses during their terms in the White House. While they were ill there was confusion about whether the vice-president should act as president and temporarily assume all the powers of that office.

The Twenty-fifth Amendment sets up a precise procedure for determining presidential disability and for giving the vice-president the full powers to serve as acting president while the president is disabled.

AMENDMENT 26 (adopted in 1971)

Section 1. *The right of citizens of the United States, who are eighteen years of age or older, to vote shall not be denied or abridged by the United States or by any State on account of age.*

Section 2. *The Congress shall have power to enforce this article by appropriate legislation.*

Before the Twenty-sixth Amendment went into operation, only four states permitted citizens under the age of twenty-one to vote. They were Georgia and Kentucky (age eighteen), Alaska (age nineteen), and Hawaii (age twenty). The Twenty-sixth Amendment, which allows eighteen-year-olds to vote in all federal and state elections, was ratified in record time.

Congress took final action on the amendment on March 23, 1971, and it was ratified by the required number of states on July 1 of the same year.

*   *   *   *   *

Beginning with the Eighteenth Amendment, Congress has customarily required ratification within seven years from the time an amendment is submitted to the states. In recent years two constitutional amendments were proposed by Congress, but they were unable to secure ratification by three-fourths of the states within the required time limit.

One of these amendments would have permitted the District of Columbia to be treated as if it were a state for the purpose of representation in Congress. This amendment would have given the District of Columbia two senators and one member of the House of Representatives. (The District of Columbia now has only a nonvoting delegate in the House.) But the amendment designed to give the District of Columbia representation in Congress failed to secure ratification by enough states before the time limit expired in August 1985.

The other recent amendment that passed in Congress but was not ratified by the necessary thirty-eight states was called the Equal Rights Amendment. It provided: "equality of rights under the law shall not be denied or abridged by the United States or by any State on account of sex." The original deadline for the ratification of the ERA was March 22, 1979, but its supporters asked for more time, so Congress extended the deadline to June 30, 1982. Even with this extension of time, only thirty-five states ratified the controversial amendment, so the ERA fell three states short of being added to the Constitution. Some champions of women's rights vow they have not given up the fight for the ERA, but they must begin all over again the process of having the amendment proposed by two-thirds of the members of both houses of Congress and ratified by three-fourths of the states.

Other possible amendments to the Constitution are receiving widespread attention in the news media. A large segment of the American public supports an amendment that would reverse a Supreme Court decision and permit organized prayers on public school property for children attending public schools. Another highly publicized possible amendment also would overrule a Supreme Court decision. It would prohibit, or allow the states to prohibit, all abortions except when necessary to save the mother's life.

Some suggested amendments deal with political changes. One of them would abolish the electoral college and replace it with a direct election by the people to select the president and vice-president. Another proposal would compel the political parties to hold a single national presidential primary election. It would bypass political conventions and permit the voters in each party to choose their presidential candidates.

Former President Jimmy Carter is among the supporters of an amendment to change the president's term of office from four years to six and make the president ineligible for reelection. This would give the chief executive more time to establish policies and perform presidential duties without being diverted by a long, strenuous reelection campaign. On the other hand, it would prohibit the voters from deciding whether they want to keep the same president in office after a four-year term.

Throughout our nation's history only Congress has officially proposed constitutional amendments for consideration by the states. There is another method, however, that can be used for proposing amendments. Article V of the Constitution provides that if two-thirds of the states request a national constitutional convention for the purpose of proposing an amendment, Congress must honor this request. If this happens, it will be something entirely new for the United States.

Twice in this century our country has come very close to having another constitutional convention—the only one since the Founding Fathers met at Philadelphia in the summer of 1787! The first time was in the 1960s, after the Supreme Court had ruled in a number of cases that the states must draw the boundaries of their election districts in such a way that each district would have approximately the same number of people. The Court first applied this principle (which came to be known as one-person, one-vote) to congressional districts and later to both houses of state legislatures. These Court rulings angered many people who felt that one house of a state legislature could be apportioned on some basis other than population. They pointed out that Congress itself has only one house based on population.

A substantial number of senators and representatives in Congress opposed the Court's one-person, one-vote decisions. In 1965 Senator Everett M. Dirksen of Illinois introduced a constitutional amendment that would have allowed states to apportion one of their two legislative houses on a basis other than population, such as geography and political subdivisions, "in order to insure effective representation in the state's legislature of the various groups and interests making up the electorate." The Dirksen amendment passed in the Senate by a vote of fifty-seven to thirty-nine, but it lacked by seven votes the necessary two-thirds majority.

Supporters of the Dirksen amendment then took their case to the states. They urged state legislatures to request Congress to call a constitutional convention for the purpose of considering this amendment. By the end of 1968 thirty-two of the necessary thirty-four states had petitioned Congress to call the convention. The Iowa legislature voted in 1969 to join the list, bringing the total to thirty-three states, just one short of the needed thirty-four. But then the momentum stalled, and the convention was never called.

More recently, many state legislatures petitioned Congress for a constitutional convention to consider an amendment requiring the national government to have a balanced budget. (A balanced budget is one in which the government spends no more money than the amount it takes in from taxation and other sources.) By 1985 thirty-two of the necessary thirty-four states had requested such a convention.

Opponents of another constitutional convention fear that it would not necessarily be limited to consideration of a single subject, such as a balanced budget. They maintain that there is little or no historical or constitutional guidance regarding the powers and scope of such a convention, so it possibly could become a "runaway" convention that might impair our basic institutions and freedoms. Those who oppose a second constitutional convention claim that its delegates might try to change or eliminate various parts of the Constitution, including the Bill of Rights and the Fourteenth Amendment. And they contend that the mere act of convening the convention would send tremors that would be felt throughout the world by friends and foes alike who regard the United States as a strong and stable government.

Additional amendments to the Constitution undoubtedly will be proposed in the years ahead. This is to be expected as new problems and different situations develop. James Madison pointed out the need for a flexible form of government when he wrote, "In framing a system which we wish to last for ages, we should not lose sight of the changes which ages will produce."

*   *   *   *   *

William Gladstone, the famous British prime minister, called the United States Constitution "the most wonderful work ever struck off at a given time by the brain and purpose of man." Perhaps he was right. Two thousand years of political theorizing and practical experience crystallized in Philadelphia in the summer of 1787 in the creation of a brilliant framework of government that has survived all the ravages of time. What fifty-five men did during that hot, humid summer in Philadelphia is probably the most significant single event in our long political history, towering above all the other remarkable achievements of the American people.

But the product of their labor could not be entering its third century as the supreme law of the land if it did not have the capacity to evolve and expand. Thomas Jefferson caught the vision of a dynamic, living Constitution when he wrote during our nation's infancy:

"Some men look at constitutions with sanctimonious reverence and deem them . . . too sacred to be touched. They ascribe to men of the preceding age a wisdom more than human, and suppose what they did to be beyond amendment. . . .

"But . . . laws and institutions must go hand in hand with the human mind. As that becomes more enlightened, as new discoveries are made, new truths disclosed, institutions must advance also, and keep pace with the times. [Otherwise,] we might as well require a man to wear still the coat which fitted him as a boy. . . ."

Appendix

Constitution of the United States of America

Boldface introductory headings and bracketed explanatory matter have been inserted to assist the reader and are not part of the Constitution. Passages that are no longer operative are in italics

PREAMBLE

We the people of the United States, in order to form a more perfect union, establish justice, insure domestic tranquillity, provide for the common defense, promote the general welfare, and secure the blessings of liberty to ourselves and our posterity, do ordain and establish this Constitution for the United States of America.

ARTICLE I. LEGISLATIVE DEPARTMENT

Section I. Congress

Legislative power vested in a two-house Congress. All legislative powers herein granted shall be vested in a Congress of the United States, which shall consist of a Senate and a House of Representatives.

Section II. House of Representatives

1. The people elect representatives every two years. The House of Representatives shall be composed of members chosen every second year by the people of the several States, and the electors [voters] in each state have the qualifications requisite for electors of the most numerous branch of the State Legislatures.

2. Qualifications of representatives. No person shall be a Representative who shall not have attained to the age of twenty-five years, and been seven years a citizen of the United States, and who shall not, when elected, be an inhabitant of that State in which he shall be chosen.

3. Representation in the House based on population. Representatives and direct taxes shall be apportioned among the several States which may be included within this Union, according to their respective numbers, *which shall be determined by adding to the whole number of free persons, including those bound to service for a term of years* [apprentices and indentured servants], *and excluding Indians not taxed, three-fifths of all other persons* [slaves]. The actual enumeration [census] shall be made within three years after the first meeting of the Congress of the United States, and within every subsequent term of ten years, in such manner as they shall by law direct. *The number of Representatives shall not exceed one for every thirty-thousand, but* each State shall have at least one Representative; *and until such enumeration shall be made, the State of New Hampshire shall be entitled to choose three, Massachusetts eight, Rhode Island and Providence Plantations one, Connecticut five, New York six, New Jersey four, Pennsylvania eight, Delaware one, Maryland six, Virginia ten, North Carolina five, South Carolina five, and Georgia three.*

4. Vacancies in the House are filled by election. When vacancies happen in the representation from any State, the Executive authority [governor] thereof shall issue writs of election [call a special election] to fill such vacancies.

5. The House selects its Speaker; has sole power to bring impeachment charges (indictments). The House of Representatives shall choose their Speaker and other officers; and shall have the sole power of impeachment.

Section III. Senate

1. Number and term of senators. The Senate of the United States shall be composed of two Senators from each State, *chosen by the legislature thereof,* for six years; and each Senator shall have one vote.

2. One-third of senators chosen every two years; vacancies (modified by Seventeenth Amendment). *Immediately after they shall be assembled in consequence of the first election, they shall be divided as* *equally as may be into three classes. The seats of the Senators of the first class shall be vacated at the expiration of the second year, and of the second class at the expiration of the fourth year, and of the third class at the expiration of the sixth year,* so that one-third may be chosen every second year; and if vacancies happen by resignation or otherwise, *during the recess of the legislature of any State,* the Executive [governor] thereof may make temporary appointments *until the next meeting of the legislature, which shall then fill such vacancies.*

3. Qualifications of senators. No person shall be a Senator who shall not have attained to the age of thirty years, and been nine years a citizen of the United States, and who shall not, when elected, be an inhabitant of that State for which he shall be chosen.

4. The vice-president presides over the Senate. The Vice-President of the United States shall be President of the Senate, but shall have no vote, unless they be equally divided [tied].

5. The Senate chooses its other officers. The Senate shall choose their other officers, and also a President *pro tempore,* in the absence of the Vice-President, or when he shall exercise the office of President of the United States.

6. The Senate has sole power to try impeachments. The Senate shall have the sole power to try all impeachments. When sitting for that purpose, they shall be on oath or affirmation. When the President of the United States is tried, the Chief Justice shall preside: and no person shall be convicted without the concurrence of two-thirds of the members present.

7. Penalties for impeachment conviction. Judgment in cases of impeachment shall not extend further than to removal from office, and disqualification to hold and enjoy any office of honor, trust or profit under the United States: but the party convicted shall nevertheless be liable and subject to indictment, trial, judgment and punishment, according to law.

Section IV. Election and Meeting of Congress

1. Election of members of Congress. The times, places and manner of holding elections for Senators and Representatives shall be prescribed in each State by the legislature thereof; but the Congress may at any time by law make or alter such regulations, except as to the places of choosing Senators.

2. Congress must meet once a year. The Congress shall assemble at least once in every year, and such meeting *shall be on the first Monday in December, unless they shall by law appoint a different day.*

Section V. Powers and Duties of Each House of Congress

1. Each house may reject members; quorums. Each house shall be the judge of the elections, returns and qualifications of its own members, and a majority of each shall constitute a quorum to do business; but a smaller number may adjourn from day to day, and may be authorized to compel the attendance of absent members, in such manner, and under such penalties, as each house may provide.

2. Each house makes its own rules. Each house may determine the rules of its proceedings, punish its members for disorderly behavior, and with the concurrence of two-thirds, expel a member.

3. Each house must keep and publish a journal of its proceedings. Each house shall keep a journal of its proceedings, and from time to time publish the same, excepting such parts as may in their judgment require secrecy; and the yeas and nays of the members of either house on any question shall, at the desire of one-fifth of those present, be entered on the journal.

4. Both houses must agree on adjournment. Neither house, during the session of Congress, shall, without the consent of the other, adjourn for more than three days, nor to any other place than that in which the two houses shall be sitting.

Section VI. Compensation and Privileges of Members of Congress; Prohibitions

1. Congressional salaries; privileges. The Senators and Representatives shall receive a compensation for their services, to be ascertained by law and paid out of the treasury of the United States. They shall in all cases except treason, felony and breach of the peace, be privileged from arrest during their attendance at the session of their respective houses, and in going to and returning from the same; and for any speech or debate in either house, they shall not be questioned in any other place.

2. A member of Congress may not hold any other federal civil office. No Senator or Representative shall, during the time for which he was elected, be appointed to any civil office under the authority of the United States, which shall have been created, or the emoluments whereof shall have been increased, during such time; and no person holding any office under the United States shall be a member of either house during his continuance in office.

Section VII. Method of Making Laws

1. Money bills must originate in the House. All bills for raising revenue shall originate in the House of Representatives; but the Senate may propose or concur with amendments as on other bills.

2. The president's veto power; Congress may override. Every bill which shall have passed the House of Representatives and the Senate, shall, before it become a law, be presented to the President of the United States; if he approve he shall sign it, but if not he shall return it with his objections to that house in which it shall have originated, who shall enter the objections at large on their journal, and proceed to reconsider it. If after such reconsideration two-thirds of that house shall agree to pass the bill, it shall be sent, together with the objections, to the other house, by which it shall likewise be reconsidered, and, if approved by two-thirds of that house, it shall become law. But in all such cases the votes of both houses shall be determined by yeas and nays, and the names of the persons voting for and against the bill shall be entered on the journal of each house respectively. If any bill shall not be returned by the President within ten days (Sundays excepted) after it shall have been presented to him, the same shall be a law, in like manner as if he had signed it, unless the Congress by their adjournment prevent its return, in which case it shall not be a law [this is the so-called pocket veto].

3. All measures requiring the agreement of both houses go to president for approval. Every order, resolution, or vote to which the concurrence of the Senate and House of Representatives may be necessary (except on a question of adjournment) shall be presented to the President of the United States; and before the same shall take effect, shall be approved by him, or being disapproved by him, shall be repassed by two-thirds of the Senate and House of Representatives, according to the rules and limitations prescribed in the case of a bill.

Section VIII. Powers Granted to Congress

Congress has certain enumerated powers:

1. It may levy and collect taxes. The Congress shall have power to lay and collect taxes, duties, imposts, and excises, to pay the debts and provide for the common defense and general welfare of the United States; but all duties, imposts and excises shall be uniform throughout the United States;

2. It may borrow money. To borrow money on the credit of the United States;

3. It may regulate foreign and interstate commerce. To regulate commerce with foreign nations, and among the several States, and with the Indian tribes;

4. It may pass naturalization and bankruptcy laws. To establish an uniform rule of naturalization, and uniform laws on the subject of bankruptcies throughout the United States;

5. It may coin money. To coin money, regulate the value thereof, and of foreign coin, and fix the standard of weights and measures;

6. It may punish counterfeiters. To provide for the punishment of counterfeiting the securities and current coin of the United States;

7. It may establish post offices. To establish post offices and post roads;

8. It may issue patents and copyrights. To promote the progress of science and useful arts by securing for limited times to authors and inventors the exclusive right to their respective writings and discoveries;

9. It may establish inferior courts. To constitute tribunals inferior to the Supreme Court;

10. It may punish crimes committed on the high seas. To define and punish piracies and felonies committed on the high seas [i.e., outside the three-mile limit] and offenses against the law of nations [international law];

11. It may declare war. To declare war, grant letters of marque and reprisal, and make rules concerning captures on land and water;

12. It may maintain an army. To raise and support armies, but no appropriation of money to that use shall be for a longer term than two years;

13. It may maintain a navy. To provide and maintain a navy;

14. It may regulate the army and navy. To make rules for the government and regulation of the land and naval forces;

15. It may call out the state militia. To provide for calling forth the militia to execute the laws of the Union, suppress insurrections, and repel invasions;

16. It shares with the states control of militias. To provide for organizing, arming, and disciplining the militia, and for governing such part of them as may be employed in the service of the United States, reserving to the States respectively the appointment of the officers, and the authority of training the militia according to the discipline prescribed by Congress;

17. It makes laws for the District of Columbia and other federal areas. To exercise exclusive legislation in all cases whatsoever, over such district (not exceeding ten miles square) as may, by cession of particular States, and the acceptance of Congress, become the seat of government of the United States, and to exercise like authority over all places purchased by the consent of the legislature of the State, in which the same shall be, for the erection of forts, magazines, arsenals, dock-yards, and other needful buildings;—and

Congress has certain implied powers:

18. It makes laws necessary for carrying out the enumerated powers. To make all laws which shall be necessary and proper for carrying into execution the foregoing powers, and all other powers vested by this Constitution in the government of the United States, or any department or officer thereof.

Section IX. Limitation on Powers Granted

1. Congress cannot control slave trade until 1808. *The migration or importation of such persons as any of the States now existing shall think proper to admit shall not be prohibited by the Congress prior to the year 1808; but a tax or duty may be imposed on such importation, not exceeding $10.00 for each person.*

2. The writ of habeas corpus may be suspended only if public safety requires it. The privilege of the writ of habeas corpus shall not be suspended, unless when in cases of rebellion or invasion the public safety may require it.

3. Attainders and ex post facto laws are prohibited. No bill or attainder or ex post facto law shall be passed.

4. Direct taxes must be apportioned according to population. No capitation [head or poll tax], or other direct, tax shall be laid, unless in proportion to the census or enumeration herein before directed to be taken.

5. Export taxes are prohibited. No tax or duty shall be laid on articles exported from any State.

6. Congress must not show preference among states in regulating commerce. No preference shall be given by any regulation of commerce or revenue to the ports of one State over those of another; nor shall vessels bound to, or from, one State, be obliged to enter, clear, or pay duties in another.

7. Treasury money may not be spent without congressional appropriation; accounting. No money shall be drawn from the treasury, but

in consequence of appropriations made by law; and a regular statement and account of the receipts and expenditures of all public
money shall be published from time to time.

8. Titles of nobility are prohibited; foreign gifts. No title of nobility
shall be granted by the United States: and no person holding any
office of profit or trust under them, shall, without the consent of the
Congress, accept of any present, emolument, office, or title, of any
kind whatever, from any king, prince, or foreign state.

Section X. Powers Prohibited to the States

1. The states are forbidden to take certain actions. No State shall
enter into any treaty, alliance, or confederation; grant letters of
marque and reprisal [i.e., authorize privateers]; coin money; emit
bills of credit [issue paper money]; make anything but gold and silver coin a [legal] tender in payment of debts; pass any bill of attainder, ex post facto, or law impairing the obligation of contracts,
or grant any title of nobility.

2. The states may not levy duties without the consent of Congress.
No State shall, without the consent of the Congress, lay any imposts
or duties on imports or exports, except what may be absolutely necessary for executing its inspection laws: and the net produce of all
duties and imposts, laid by any State on imports or exports, shall be
for the use of the treasury of the United States; and all such laws
shall be subject to the revision and control of the Congress.

**3. Certain other federal powers are denied the states except with the
consent of Congress.** No State shall, without the consent of Congress, lay any duty of tonnage [i.e., duty on ship tonnage], keep
[nonmilitia] troops or ships of war in time of peace, enter into any
agreement or compact with another State, or with a foreign power,
or engage in war, unless actually invaded, or in such imminent danger as will not admit of delay.

ARTICLE II. EXECUTIVE DEPARTMENT

Section I. President and Vice-President

1. Executive power vested in president: term of office. The executive
power shall be vested in a President of the United States of America. He shall hold his office during the term of four years, and,
together with the Vice-President, chosen for the same term, be elected as follows:

2. The appointment and number of presidential electors. Each State shall appoint, in such manner as the legislature thereof may direct, a number of electors, equal to the whole number of Senators and Representatives to which the State may be entitled in the Congress; but no Senator or Representative, or person holding an office of trust or profit under the United States, shall be appointed an elector.

3. Method of electing the President and Vice-President (modified by Twelfth Amendment). *The electors shall meet in their respective States, and vote by ballot for two persons, of whom one at least shall not be an inhabitant of the same State with themselves. And they shall make a list of all the persons voted for, and of the number of votes for each; which list they shall sign and certify, and transmit sealed to the seat of government of the United States, directed to the President of the Senate. The President of the Senate shall, in the presence of the Senate and House of Representatives, open all the certificates, and the votes shall then be counted. The person having the greatest number of votes shall be the President, if such number be a majority of the whole number of electors appointed; and if there be more than one who have such majority, and have an equal number of votes, then the House of Representatives shall immediately choose by ballot one of them for President; and if no person have a majority, then from the five highest on the list the said house shall in like manner choose the President. But in choosing the President the votes shall be taken by States, the representation from each State having one vote; a quorum for this purpose shall consist of a member or members from two-thirds of the States, and a majority of all the States shall be necessary to a choice. In every case, after the choice of the President, the person having the greatest number of votes of the electors shall be the Vice-President. But if there should remain two or more who have equal votes, the Senate shall choose from them by ballot the Vice-President.*

4. Congress decides when electors are chosen and when they vote. The Congress may determine the time of choosing the electors and the day on which they shall give their votes; which day shall be the same throughout the United States.

5. Qualifications of the president. No person except a natural-born citizen, *or a citizen of the United States at the time of the adoption of this Constitution,* shall be eligible to the office of President; neither shall any person be eligible to that office who shall not have attained to the age of thirty-five years, and been fourteen years a resident within the United States [i.e., a legal resident].

6. Presidential succession (modified by Twenty-fifth Amendment). In case of the removal of the President from office or of his death, resignation, or inability to discharge the powers and duties of the said office, the same shall devolve on the Vice-President, and the Congress may by law provide for the case of removal, death, resignation, or inability, both of the President and Vice-President, declaring what officer shall then act as President, and such officer shall act accordingly, until the disability be removed, or a President shall be elected.

7. The president's salary. The President shall, at stated times, receive for his services a compensation, which shall neither be increased nor diminished during the period for which he shall have been elected, and he shall not receive within that period any other emolument from the United States, or any of them.

8. The president's oath of office. Before he enter on the execution of his office, he shall take the following oath or affirmation:—"I do solemnly swear (or affirm) that I will faithfully execute the office of the President of the United States, and will to the best of my ability preserve, protect and defend the Constitution of the United States."

Section II. Powers of the President

1. The president has military and civil powers. The President shall be commander in chief of the army and navy of the United States, and of the militia of the several States, when called into the actual service of the United States; he may require the opinion, in writing, of the principal officer in each of the executive departments, upon any subject relating to the duties of the respective offices, and he shall have power to grant reprieves and pardons for offenses against the United States, except in cases of impeachment.

2. The president may negotiate treaties and appoint federal officials. He shall have power, by and with the advice and consent of the Senate, to make treaties, provided two-thirds of the Senators present concur; and he shall nominate, and by and with the advice and consent of the Senate, shall appoint ambassadors, other public ministers and consuls, judges of the Supreme Court, and all other officers of the United States, whose appointments are not herein otherwise provided for, and which shall be established by law: but the Congress may by law vest the appointment of such inferior officers, as they think proper, in the President alone, in the courts of law, or in the heads of departments.

3. The president may fill vacancies during Senate recess. The President shall have power to fill up all vacancies that may happen during the recess of the Senate, by granting commissions which shall expire at the end of their next session.

Section III. Other Powers and Duties of the President

Messages to Congress; receive ambassadors; execution of the laws. He shall from time to time give to the Congress information of the state of the Union, and recommend to their consideration such measures as he shall judge necessary and expedient; he may, on extraordinary occasions, convene both houses, or either of them, and in case of disagreement between them, with respect to the time of adjournment, he may adjourn them to such time as he shall think proper; he shall receive ambassadors and other public ministers; he shall take care that the laws be faithfully executed, and shall commission all the officers of the United States.

Section IV. Removal of Executive and Civil Officers

Civil officers may be removed by impeachment. The President, Vice-President and all civil officers of the United States shall be removed from office on impeachment for, and on conviction of, treason, bribery, or other high crimes and misdemeanors.

ARTICLE III. JUDICIAL DEPARTMENT

Section I. The Federal Courts

The judicial power vested in the federal courts. The judicial power of the United States shall be vested in one Supreme Court, and in such inferior courts as the Congress may from time to time ordain and establish. The Judges, both of the Supreme and inferior courts, shall hold their offices during good behavior, and shall, at stated times, receive for their services a compensation which shall not be diminished during their continuance in office.

Section II. Jurisdiction of Federal Courts

1. Cases that may come before federal courts. The judicial power shall extend to all cases, in law and equity, arising under this Constitution, the laws of the United States, and treaties made, or which shall be made, under this authority;—to all cases of admiralty and maritime jurisdiction;—to controversies to which the United States

shall be a party;—to controversies between two or more States;—
between a State and citizens of another State;—between citizens of
different States;—between citizens of the same State claiming lands
under grants of different States, and between a State, or the citizens
thereof, and foreign states, citizens or subjects.

2. Jurisdiction of the Supreme Court. In all cases affecting ambassadors, other public ministers and consuls, and those in which a
State shall be party, the Supreme Court shall have original jurisdiction. In all other cases before mentioned, the Supreme Court shall
have appellate jurisdiction, both as to law and fact, with such exceptions, and under such regulations, as the Congress shall make.

3. Trial for federal crime is by jury. The trial of all crimes, except in
cases of impeachment, shall be by jury; and such trial shall be held
in the State where the said crimes shall have been committed; but
when not committed within any State, the trial shall be at such place
or places as the Congress may by law have directed.

Section III. Treason

1. Treason defined. Treason against the United States shall consist
only in levying war against them, or in adhering to their enemies,
giving them aid and comfort. No person shall be convicted of treason unless on the testimony of two witnesses to the same overt act,
or on confession in open court.

2. Congress decides punishment for treason. The Congress shall
have power to declare the punishment of treason, but no attainder
of treason shall work corruption of blood, or forfeiture except during the life of the person attainted.

ARTICLE IV. THE STATES AND THE FEDERAL GOVERNMENT

Section I. Official Acts of the States

Each state must respect the public acts of other states. Full faith and
credit shall be given in each State to the public acts, records, and
judicial proceedings of every other State. And the Congress may by
general laws prescribe the manner in which such acts, records, and
proceedings shall be proved, and the effect thereof.

Section II. Duties of States to States

1. Citizenship in one state is valid in all. The citizens of each State shall be entitled to all privileges and immunities of citizens in the several States.

2. Fugitives from justice must be returned to the state from which they have fled. A person charged in any State with treason, felony, or other crime, who shall flee from justice, and be found in another State, shall on demand of the executive authority [governor] of the State from which he fled, be delivered up, to be removed to the State having jurisdiction of the crime.

3. Slaves and apprentices must be returned (invalidated by the Thirteenth Amendment). *No person held to service or labor in one State, under the laws thereof, escaping into another, shall, in consequence of any law or regulation therein, be discharged from such service or labor, but shall be delivered up on claim of the party to whom such service or labor may be due.*

Section III. New States and Territories

1. Congress may admit new states. New States may be admitted by the Congress into this Union; but no new State shall be formed or erected within the jurisdiction of any other State; nor any State be formed by the junction of two or more States, or parts of States, without the consent of the legislatures of the States concerned as well as of the Congress.

2. Congress regulates federal territory and property. The Congress shall have power to dispose of and make all needful rules and regulations respecting the territory or other property belonging to the United States; and nothing in this Constitution shall be so construed as to prejudice any claims of the United States, or of any particular State.

Section IV. Protection to the States

United States guarantees to states representative government and protection against invasion and rebellion. The United States shall guarantee to every State in this Union a republican form of government, and shall protect each of them against invasion; and on application of the legislature, or of the executive [governor] (when the legislature cannot be convened), against domestic violence.

ARTICLE V. THE PROCESS OF AMENDMENT

The Constitution may be amended in four ways. The Congress, whenever two-thirds of both houses shall deem it necessary, shall propose amendments to this Constitution, or, on the application of the legislatures of two-thirds of the several States, shall call a convention for proposing amendments, which, in either case, shall be valid to all intents and purposes, as part of this Constitution, when ratified by the legislatures of three-fourths of the several States, or by conventions in three-fourths thereof, as the one or the other mode of ratification may be proposed by the Congress; *provided that no amendments which may be made prior to the year one thousand eight hundred and eight shall in any manner affect the first and fourth clauses in the ninth section of the first article,* and that no State, without its consent, shall be deprived of its equal suffrage in the Senate.

ARTICLE VI. GENERAL PROVISIONS

1. The debts of the Confederation are taken over. All debts contracted and engagements entered into, before the adoption of this Constitution, shall be as valid against the United States under this Constitution, as under the Confederation.

2. The Constitution, federal laws, and treaties are the supreme law of the land. This Constitution, and the laws of the United States which shall be made in pursuance thereof; and all treaties made, or which shall be made, under the authority of the United States, shall be the supreme law of the land; and the judges in every State shall be bound thereby, anything in the Constitution or laws of any State to the contrary notwithstanding.

3. Federal and state officers must take an oath to support the Constitution. The Senators and Representatives before mentioned, and the members of the several State legislatures, and all executive and judicial officers, both of the United States and of the several States, shall be bound by oath or affirmation to support this Constitution; but no religious test shall ever be required as a qualification to any office or public trust under the United States.

ARTICLE VIII. RATIFICATION OF THE CONSTITUTION

The Constitution becomes effective when ratified by conventions in nine states. The ratification of the conventions of nine States shall be sufficient for the establishment of this Constitution between the States so ratifying the same.

Done in Convention by the unanimous consent of the States present, the seventeenth day of September in the year of our Lord one thousand seven hundred and eighty-seven and of the Independence of the United States of America the twelfth. In witness whereof we have hereunto subscribed our names.

[Signed by]   G° Washington
                                  President and Deputy from Virginia
                                     [and thirty-eight others]

(The Amendments to the Constitution are on pages 102-108 and 115-134.)

Further Reading

Adair, Douglas. *Fame and the Founding Fathers*. New York: Norton, 1974.

Bailyn, Bernard. *The Ideological Origins of the American Revolution*. Cambridge, Mass.: Belknap, 1967.

Berger, Raoul. *Congress v. The Supreme Court* Boston: Harvard University Press, 1969 . (Paperback, New York: Bantam Books, 1973.)

Bowen, Catherine Drinker. *Miracle at Philadelphia: The Story of the Constitutional Convention, May to September 1787*. Boston: Atlantic Monthly Press, 1986.

Brant, Irving. *The Bill of Rights: Its Origin and Meaning*. Indianapolis: Bobbs-Merrill, 1965.

———. *The Fourth President: a Life of James Madison*. Indianapolis: Bobbs-Merrill, 1970.

Burns, James MacGregor. *The Vineyard of Liberty*. New York: Knopf, 1982.

Chafee, Zechariah, Jr. *Free Speech in the United States*. New York: Atheneum, 1969.

Congressional Quarterly's Guide to Congress, 2nd ed. Washington: Congressional Quarterly Inc., 1976.

Cullop, Floyd G. *The Constitution of the United States: An Introduction* (New York: New American Library, 1984).

Donovan, Frank. *Mr. Madison's Constitution: The Story Behind the Constitutional Convention*. New York: Dodd, Mead, 1965.

Fisher, Louis. *Politics of Shared Powers*. Washington: Congressional Quarterly Press, 1981.

Flexner, James Thomas. *George Washington in the American Revolution, 1775-1783*. Boston: Little, Brown, 1968.

Freeman, Douglas Southall. *George Washington, a Biography*, 7 volumes. New York: Scribner's, 1948-1957.

Friendly, Fred W. and Martha J.H. Elliott. *The Constitution: That Delicate Balance*. New York: Random House, 1984.

Green, Jack P., ed. *Colonies to Nation, 1763-1789*. New York: Norton, 1975.

Hamilton, Alexander, James Madison, and John Jay. *The Federalist Papers*, ed. with an introduction by Clinton Rossiter. New York: New American Library, 1961.

Hofstadter, Richard, ed. *Great Issues in American History: From the Revolution to the Civil War, 1765-1865*. New York: Vintage, 1958.

Jefferson, Thomas. *Writings*. Merrill Peterson, ed. New York: Library of America, 1983.

Jensen, Merrill. *The New Nation: A History of the United States During the Confederation, 1781-1789*. New York: Vintage Books, 1965.

Koch, Adrienne. *Madison's Advice to My Country*. Princeton, N.J.: Princeton University Press, 1966.

Lawson, Don. *The Changing Face of the Constitution*. New York: Watts, 1979.

Liston, Robert A. *Tides of Justice: The Supreme Court and the Constitution in Our Time*. New York: Delacorte, 1966.

Lomask, Milton. *The Spirit of 1787: The Making of Our Constitution*. New York: Farrar Straus Giroux, 1980.

McDonald, Forrest. *Alexander Hamilton*. New York: Norton, 1979.

———. *Enough Wise Men: The Story of Our Constitution*. New York: Putnam's, 1970.

McGee, Dorothy Horton. *Framers of the Constitution*. New York: Dodd, Mead, 1968.

Madison, James. *Notes on the Debates in the Federal Convention of 1787*. Adrienne Koch, ed. Athens, Ohio: Ohio Universtiy Press, 1966.

Morris, Richard B. *Witnesses at the Creation*. New York: Holt, Rinehart and Winston, 1985.

Nevins, Allan. *The American States During and After the Revolution, 1775-1789*. New York: A.M. Kelley, 1969.

Pyle, Christopher H. and Richard M. Pious. *The President, Congress, and the Constitution*. New York: The Free Press, 1984 .

Rossiter, Clinton. *1787: The Grand Convention*. New York: Macmillan, 1966.

Silverman, Kenneth. *A Cultural History of the American Revolution*. New York: Crowell, 1976.

Smith, Page. *The Constitution*. New York: Morrow, 1980.

———. *The Shaping of America*, Volume 3. New York: McGraw-Hill, 1980.

Stiles, Francis N. *John Marshall: Defender of the Constitution*. Boston: Little, Brown, 1981.

The Supreme Court and Individual Rights. Washington: Congressional Quarterly Inc., 1980.

Tuchman, Barbara W. "The British Lose America," Part 4 of *The March of Folly: From Troy to Vietnam*. New York: Knopf, 1984.

Van Doren, Carl. *The Great Rehearsal*. New York: Viking, 1948.

Wood, Gordon S. *The Creation of the American Republic*, 1776-1787. New York: Norton, 1972.

Index